Readings in Information Science and Information Technology

Readings in Information Science and Information Technology

Prof. Dr. G Devarajan
UGC Emeritus Fellow
Dept.of Library & Information Science
University of Kerala, Trivandrum

Ess Ess Publications
New Delhi

Readings in Information Science and Information Technology

ISBN : 978-81-7000-627-5

Rs.475/-

First Published 2011

Published by:
Ess Ess Publications
4837/24, Ansari Road,
Darya Ganj,
New Delhi-110 002.
INDIA
Phones: 23260807, 41563444
Fax: 41563334
E-mail: info@essessreference.com
www.essessreference.com

Cover Design by *Patch Creative Unit*

Printed and bound in India at Salasar Imaging Systems.

Contents

Preface

This book is a collection of selected studies on various aspects in Information Science and Information Technology. The topics are important since they represent live issues and problems that arise in practical information management. The areas include, the concept of Information Science and Information technology, Information and knowledge management, information literacy , sociology of information, socio-economic factors and reading interest, I.T application in higher education, digital divide and digital libraries, library software packages, I.T in LIS curriculum and guidelines and parameters in qualitative research etc. The topics are of academic relevance as they figure in the syllabi of Library and Information Science courses in India. The book would prove to be of interest to teachers and students of Library and Information Science at all levels and practicing librarians and information managers of all types of libraries and Information centres. A bibliography and book index are given as auxiliaries for further reading and effective use of the book. It is hoped that this book will be well received by the academic and professional communities in the field of Information Science and Information Technology.

I express my sincere gratitude to Mr. Sumit Sethi,

M/s Ess Ess Publications, New Delhi who has brought out the book with their customary promptness in an attractive format.

Prof. Dr. G. Devarajan

Trivandrum

Chapter 1

Information, Information Science and Information Technology

INTRODUCTION

Information is a vital resource in today's society which hardly needs emphasis as it brings people and thought together .It is considered as the fourth resource , the other three being people, money and physical resources. It is also considered as fifth basic human needs in the order, air, water, food and shelter. It is an indispensable raw material for right decision-making from governmental level to the personal level. It is a well accepted generalization that a country which is rich in information is rich in the socio-economic spheres. Information is dividing the world between fast moving economies that make effective use of information and slow moving economies that do not use it. The backwardness of any country in respect of socio-economic spheres is mainly due to lack of adequate information especially in the field of Science and technology. The significance of information paved the way for development of Science information and technologies to manage information. In fact information has a synergizing effect in a number of human activities in the educational, scientific, technological and societal spheres. Thus one can realize that information is an all pervasive resource and helps in establishing a continuum from the past to present and finally to the future. In this chapter an attempt is made to discuss the concepts Information, Information Science , Information technology Informatics in their various ramifications.

INFORMATION

The word 'information' is derived from Latin word, "Informare" means to give shape to something. There are a number of terms such as knowledge, facts, data, news, message etc used in common parlance as synonyms or near synonyms to 'information'. But none of these terms are equivalent to information. In fact it is very difficult to define information precisely. According to the Oxford English Dictionary: i)Information is the action of informing; formation or moulding the mind or character, training, instruction, teaching; communication of instructive knowledge; ii) the action of informing; communication of the knowledge of "news" of some fact or occurrence; the action of telling or fact of being told of something; and iii) knowledge communicated concerning some particular fact, subject or event; that of which one is apprised or told; intelligence, news. Van Nostrand's Scientific Encyclopedia gives the concept of information as "a collection of facts or other data especially as derived from the processing of data" Whereas, it is an assemblage of data in a comprehensible form recorded on paper or some other medium, and capable of communication. A number of authors have attempted to define information. According to Shera, information, both in the sense it is used by the biologists and in the sense librarians use it, is a "fact". It is the stimuli we receive through our senses. It may be an isolated fact or a whole cluster of facts; but it is still a unit; it is a unit of thought. In the words of prof. Bhattacharyya, information is the message conveyed or intended to be conveyed by a systematised body of ideas, or its accepted or acceptable substitutes. Information is the meaning that a human expresses by, or extracts from, representation of facts and ideas by means of the known conventions of the representation used. According to Faibisoff and Dely "information is an idea. It is a symbol or a set of symbols which have the potential for meaning".

Information can be defined as "some meaningful message recorded in conventional or non conventional media and stored and processed by messages and their dissemination to users". As Mcpherson states that information permeates all organizations, it is the raw metatarsal of cognitive activity.... the means whereby organization obtains its window on the world. In fact it is a diffused resource. Horton defines information in the context of treating it as a resource:

- Something of fundamental value, like money, capital goods, labour or raw materials;
- Something with specifiable and measurable characteristics, such as method of collection, utilities and uses, a life cycle pattern with different attributes at each stage, and interchangeability with other resources;
- An input , which can be transferred into useful outputs;
- Something that presents to top management a variety of development choices.

McGarry has tried to provide the varied attributes of 'information' rather than defining information. He provides the following attributes to information. i) Information can be regarded as a near synonym of fact. ii) It has a transforming or reinforcing effect on what is known or believed to be known by a human being; iii) Information is used as an aid in decision making; iv) Information is the freedom of choice one has in selecting message; v) Information is a necessary piece of "something" when we are faced with a choice. The amount required depends upon the complexity of the decision to be made; vi) Information is the raw material from which knowledge is derived; vii) Information is exchanged with outer world; not merely received; and viii) Information can be defined in terms of its effect on the receipient. It is seen that a comprehensive definition of the concept 'information' is not possible due to its amorphous, slippery, complex and multifarious nature. To quote T,N.Rajan, "no universally accepted definition of information is yet crystallised perhaps it will never be crystallized."

INFORMATION, KNOWLEDGE AND WISDOM

The relationship between knowledge and information is given in the Random House Dictionary of English Language as "knowledge communicated or received concerning a particular fact or circumstance; any knowledge gained through communication, research, instruction is information. Information and knowledge are distinguished as follows:

i) Information is piecemeal, fragmented ,particular, whereas knowledge is structural, coherent and universal;

ii) Information is timely, transitory, perhaps even ephemeral, whereas knowledge is of enduring significance.

iii) Information is a flow of messages, whereas knowledge is a stock largely resulting from the flow in the sense that the input of information may affect the stock of knowledge by adding to it, restructuring it or changing it in anyway (though conceivably information may leave knowledge unchanged).

In the words of Brookes, the knowledge is a summation

of many bits of "information" which are organised into some sort of coherent entity. The relationship is represented by means of a simple equation, which Brookes calls the "fundamental equation of information Science".

$$K(s) + AI = K(S + As)$$

Here K(s) is knowledge sturcture and K(S + AS) is the modified knowledge sturcture caused by absorption of the increment of information of K(S). Brookes believes that correct solution of this equation and its proper interpretation may enable us to fully explain information process.

T.S Eliot brought the relationship between information, data, knowledge and wisdom in poetical lines as: Where is the wisdom, We have lost in knowledge? Where is the knowledge, We have lost in information? Knowledge has more profound connotation when compared with information. Knowledge can carry with it the idea that apparently objective information is filtered and conditioned in transmission, by individual life-experiences and social values. Society forms the alchemic process by which base "information" is transmuted into "knowledge". Thus a conceptual framework built up from the idea of "knowledge" will include a socio-cultural dimension which might be omitted from a framework built up from the more reductive idea of "information". However, it is accepted that, given the current popularity of the word and the fact that it is commonly used interchangeably with the word "knowledge", information is the word that is more likely to be used. Knowledge is like light. Weightless and intangible, it can easily travel the world, enlightening the lives of people everywhere.

TYPES OF INFORMATION

There are various types or forms of information. These types are recognized on the basis of different characteristic features. According to Prof,Bhattacharyya information has two recognizable varieties viz i) Discursive; and ii) Non-Discursive information. Discursive information is the message conveyed by a systematised body of ideas or its accepted or acceptable substitutes. The information that is not discursive is non-discursive information. Non-discursive information is of two types: Qualitative and quantitative information. Information can be categorised on the basis of the nature of its use and purpose for which it is used. J.H.Shera has categorised information into six types. They are: i) Conceptual information ii) empirical information iii) procedural information iv) stimulatory information v) policy information; and vi) directive information.

The social Scientists categorise information as: i) statistical information; ii) descriptive information iii) analytical information. The population data of a country can be considered example of statistical information. If someone describes the growth of population that has taken place in various years that will constitute descriptive information whereas if someone analyses and interprets the above statistical information that will result into analytical information or interpretative information.

Saracevic and Wood have categorized information based on developmental needs as : i)Scientific and technical information; ii) policy and management information; and iii) operational and industrial information. Information is categorized based on its use in various human activities such as: i)Technical information; ii)Environmental information; iii) Economic information; iv)Geographical information ; v) Climatological information ;and vi)Socio-cultural information.

QUALITIES OF INFORMATION

Information has varied attributes and qualities. Cleveland in an address to the World future Society in 1982, outlined the inherent characteristics of information. He applied the following seven objectives to qualify information: human, expandable, compressible, substitutable, transportable, diffusive and shareable. As a vital resource, information ought to have certain ideal qualities also. They are: i) Accessibility ii) Comprehensiveness; iii) Precision; iv) Compatibility; v) Timeliness; vi) Clarity; vii)Flexibility; viii)Verifiability; ix) Free of bias; and x) Quantifiable.

William F William has recognised six parameters of information. They are: a)Quantity of information which can be measured by the number of documents, pages, words, characters, bits, drawings etc; b)Content, the meaning of information; c)Structure, the organisation of information and its logical relationship between statements or elements; d)Language, symbols, alphabets, codes and syntax with which the ideas are expressed; e)Quality, that which characterizes the completeness, accuracy, relevance and timeliness of information; and f)Life, the total span of time in which value can be derived from the information.

PRINCIPLES OF INFORMATION

The basic principles of librarianship are focused in the Five laws of Library Science enunciated by Dr. S. R. Ranganathan, the luminary in the field. On the analogy of Five laws of Library Science, Prof.Bhattacharyya formulated Five principles of Information viz i)Information is for use; ii)Every information user his/her information; iii)Every piece of information its user; iv)Save the time of the information user; and v)The universe of information is ever growing. These principles underline that information should be put into active use and it should be channelised to the right user at the right time in the right form. This will ultimately result in the growth of universe of nascent information and will be helpful for all pervasive growth in all spheres of human activities.

AGENCIES OF INFORMATION GENERATION

Information is an outcome of various intellectual activities of human beings. The information generation activities are made by individuals, organisations, learned bodies and Governmental agencies. Research and developmental activities carried out by individual research and team research in R & D organisations generate quite a lot of nascent information in the fields of Science and technology, Humanities and Social Sciences. The establishment of various types of R & D institutions immediately after the Second world war all over the world geared up research activities on various subjects. In addition to research institutions a number of academic institutions like universities and colleges entered the arena of academic research which also produced a lot of information. Government is another agency which generates enormous information. Local Governments, State Governments, Central Government, Government departments etc are agencies involved in the generation of new information. These are generated as Census reports, administration reports, rules and regulations, Bills and Acts etc.

In addition to the above said agencies for generation of information, business and industrial organisations generate a lot of information in the field of various commercial sectors and industrial fields. The information generated by such agencies is used for commercial and industrial development.

MEDIA OF INFORMATION

Information is generated through a number of communication channels or media. It is transmitted through printed media viz books and periodicals and mass media viz news papers, radio, Television, cinema etc. These media disseminate a large quantity of information. In the case of printed media 20th century witnessed the exponential growth. It is calculated that the number of articles published in journals each year in the field of Science and Technology alone exceeds one million. It is estimated that literature doubles within a range of 5-10 years in Science and Technology and in a range of 7-13 years in Social Science subjects. In subjects like Computer Science the rate of doubling literature is faster i.e. 1-2 years. It is interesting to note that the growth of literature at the global level is roughly three times faster than the growth of population. In the case of mass media also growth rate is high because of extensive use of these media. It may be said that today we are living in an age of "information explosion" or "information boom" due to information overload or information flood. The major factors leading to this phenomenon are exponential growth of literature, technological developments in printing technology, revolution in the field of information technology.

The information explosion and information flood have created quite a number of problems to information managers in the management of information exhaustively, expeditiously, pin-pointedly and precisely. Of course, information explosion is an opportunity to developed countries and a threat for Third world countries. Together with information explosion we are also confronted with another problem, "information pollution". The proliferation of literature which does not contribute substantially to add knowledge, publication with erroneous information, rehash, cheap publications which exploit the weakness of the society etc. create such a problem. In fact the information users of today are in a state of "information anxiety" and in the state of drowning in information but starving for knowledge.

VALUE OR USES OF INFORMATION

Information is a valuable commodity. The value of information is determined on the basis of providing it to the right user at the right time in the right form with precision. Information is a valuable input to various types of user groups such as students, teachers, researchers, professionals, decision makers, planers etc to satisfy various types of information needs. It is an asset and like other assets and it is useless if it is not put to use. So the value of information is also determined on the basis of how it is utilized. In an information society the importance of information is paramount.

Atherton remarks on the value of information that researchers and scientists necessitates effective communication :

i) To stimulate thought and action by injection of and interaction with, other people's ideas, knowledge, experience and achievements ;

ii) To promote continuous awareness of developments;

iii) To diminish the probability of unwitting duplication of work;

iv) To provide introductory and background information for work at hand ; and

v) To meet specific requirements.

Saracevic and Wood identified the following uses or values of information. It is used for

- Decision making/planning
- Problem solving
- Knowledge competence
- Adaptation
- Productivity
- Efficient and effective use of resources
- Success
- Business
- Research and Development
- Education; and
- Self fulfillment and advancement of individuals.

INFORMATION SOCIETY

The society which depends on information for all its developments is popularly known as information society. Information societies have three main characteristics. They are i) Information is used as an economic resource. Organisations make greater use of information to increase their efficiency, to stimulate innovation and to increase their efficiency, to stimulate innovation and to increase their effectiveness and competitive position, often through improvements in the quality of the goods and services that they produce. There is also a trend towards the development of more information-intensive organisations that add greater amounts of value and thus benefit country's overall economy; ii) it is possible to identify greater use of information among the general public. People use information more intensively in their activities as consumers to inform their choices between different products, to explore their entitlements to public services, and to take greater control over their own lives. They also use information as citizens to exercise their civil rights and responsibilities; and iii) the development of an information sector within the economy. The function of the information sector is to satisfy the general demand for information facilities and services. A significant part of the sector is concerned with the technological infrastructure - the networks of telecommunications and computers.

INFORMATION AGE

Information age refers to modern times, in which getting and giving the right information is the driving force of the society . The rapid growth of the technology we use to access information has moved the world away from that of mechanization and industrialization and towards a truly global economy based on the flow of information. The information age also commonly known as the computer age or computer era is an idea that the current age will be characterized by the ability of individuals to transfer information freely and to have instant access to knowledge that would have been difficult or impossible to find previously. The idea is linked to the concept digital age or digital revolution and carries the ramifications of a shift from traditional industry that the industrial revolution brought through industrialization to an economy based on the manipulation of information.

INFORMETRICS

According to Brookes, the term Informetrics was first proposed by Otto Nacke of West Germany in 1979. An FID Committee with very broadly defined objectives in the provision of research and technical data gave this name. However, the term was not widely adopted until 1987 when B.C.Brookes at the First Conference on Bibliometrics and

Theoretical Aspects of Information Retrieval held at Belgium, suggested that the term "Informetrics" be included in the name of the Second International conference on the subject. Tague-Sutcliffe defines informetrics as "the study of the quantitative aspects of information in any form, not just records or bibliographies, and in any social group, not just scientists. It can incorporate, utilize and extend the many studies of the measurement of information that lies outside the boundaries of both Bibliometrics and Scientometrics, and she continues to say that, although in practice the scope of informetrics is very broad."

INFORMATION THEORY

Information theory is the mathematical study of the transmission ,reception, storage and retrieval of information based on the statistical analysis of communication between humans and machines. It is a branch of applied mathematics and electrical engineering involving the quantification of information . Information theory was developed by Claude E Shannon to find fundamental limits on signal processing operations such as compressing data and on reliably storing and communicating data. Since its inception it has broadened to find applications in many other areas including statistical inference , natural language processing, cryptography generally, networks other than communication networks - as in neurobiology , the evolution and function of molecular codes, model selection in ecology, thermal physics, quantum computing, plagiarism detection and other forms of data analysis.

INFORMATION AUDIT

Information Audit is a popular concept in library science literature. It is the examination and evaluation of existing information sources, services and products in an organisation, with a view to developing a strategy for their more efficient and effective preparation, promotion, use or marketing.

In its most precise sense an information audit is that process by which a physical verification and examination of the total information assets within an organization takes place, to ensure that information resources which have been acquired by an organization can be accounted for and located. It is now common practice to define the information audit much more widely, to include the initial examination of resources as described above resulting in an inventory of information resources, then building on that to explore the way in which information flows and knowledge is shared throughout an organization: the mechanisms and channels used, the information needs of the organization's members and the staffing requirement in terms of knowledge and skills to ensure that the organization's total intellectual capital is managed and exploited to maximum efficiency.

The idea of information audit is derived from financial audit in accounting , which as Ellis et al noted , are generally 'compliance' audits, undertaken to ensure that the organization is adhering to proper fiscal and legal standards in its financial management. Information audit takes more the character of 'advisory' audits, which are, more concerned with informing users of existing systems and practices and with assessing the appropriateness of existing systems, standards and practices to the organization's goal or objectives.

Becker (1990) describes five types of information audit:

i) Those based on cost-benefit model;

ii) Those that seek to map the relationship between resources;

iii) Hybrid approaches (which combine the feature of the first two)

iv) Audits management information; and

v) Operational advisory audits

It is the examination and evaluation of existing information sources, services and products in an organization, with a view to developing a strategy for their more efficient and effective preparation, promotion, use or marketing.

The use of processes such as information audits is increasingly recommended as part of the information management task. The term audit is used to indicate that the process is similar to financial audits; finding out what information exist, their value, and who is responsible for managing and exploiting them.

The information audit should be seen as a mapping process which brings together information about who the users are, what information they have access to (both from the library and from the other sources), what their information needs are and how the provision of information services can support those needs. Peter Gillman has outlined the use of information audits to identify abut user needs, and he goes into some detail the rather thorny task of separating user needs and user wants.

AIM AND PURPOSE

The information audit in its broadest sense is seen as a valuable management tool and part of continuous management review to assist in the process of achieving maximum effectiveness of information provision and use. Its invention is to establish the total information resources and knowledge base to which an organization and all its constituent part have access, of which they can make use and from which they can benefit. The information audit also offers a framework from which to develop a knowledge audit. It aims to consider not only what information is available, but also the means by which information and knowledge are gathered and disseminated throughout the organization, the systems and procedures required for this and the way in which such activities are managed and coordinated. The information audit can form the base from which an organizational information policy can develop. It also provides the platform for long term library and information services, strategic planning and service and development.

PREPARATION AND PLANNING

What will be needed in advance of the audit itself will be a clear profile of the organization, its current and planned activities and objectives, towards which any future information and knowledge management policy and operation can be directed. Each organization will be different in terms of sector, activities, objectives, structure and management style; therefore the profile will assist in the choice of audit methods and techniques to be used, the design and content of questionnaires and checklists, and the desired mix of the user sample. Those conducting the audit must identify precisely what it is necessary to investigate, drawing up appropriate checklists of items to be audited. Checklists should also cover related equipments and systems in use, their quantities and location. Questionnaires or interview schedules will have to be prepared at this stage as the basis for subsequent user and usage surveys, and consideration is given to appropriate methods of communication to be used. Decisions will also be required on the amount and type of operational statistics required in support of the final analysis and recommendations.

THE PROCESS

Following the initial planning, the first step in the information audit is to carry out a thorough investigation of the information sources and related means of access and retrieval that exist through the organization. If this involves arranging visits to other departments and offices and discussion with individuals, then it is appropriate to combine the first step with the next part of the process of users' information needs analysis.

Gathering this information requires some form of user surveys, usually either by face-to-face interview or by the circulation of a questionnaire. Both methods should take as little of the user's time as possible. This is likely to generate a greater response, as adequate preparation and understanding by all those involved. The Library and Information services website offers a useful means of publicizing the audit and confirming the schedule. In order to ensure maximum co-operation from individuals and departments, appropriate communication of its objectives will need to be made beforehand. The purpose and style of the investigation should be put forward in positive terms, emphasizing the ultimate benefits and the value of the user's participation, allowing adequate time for individuals to prepare their response . When the audit has been completed there should be feed back to those who have participated as well as wider dissemination of the results to inform senior management, whose commitment will be essential to future development.

USE AND BENEFITS

Information audits also involve reviews of systems and procedures, analysis of operations, costing and budgeting reviews, and Library and Information Service staff training and development assessment. When an organization is pursuing a quality management policy, the quality manuals and related procedures can act as a valuable source of reference, often suggesting new approaches and solutions to what might have been viewed as long standing problems.

As a management technique the information audit has a lot to offer, particularly if it is used on a regular basis, rather than as a one-off activity. It can act as a monitoring mechanism, providing regular feed back on the quality of both the information itself and its provisions; it will assist in short and long term financial and management planning; it can help to shape overall organizational policy. To achieve this will involve setting up follow-up procedures and activities to ensure: continued two-way communication with users; wider information sharing; ongoing staff development in terms of renewing skills and keeping up to date subject knowledge and sources, as well as professional practice; and continuous awareness of and involvement in the activities of the organization as a whole.

INFORMATION SCIENCE

There are a number of definitions available to explain the discipline, Science of information or information science. According to the Encyclopedia Britanica , Information Science is the discipline that deals with the processes of storing and transferring of information. It attempts to bring together concepts and methods from various disciplines such as library science, computer science, lingustics, cybernetics, and other technologies inorder to develop techniques and devices to aid in the handling -that is, in the storage, control and retrieval of information.

According to Pauline Atherton Information Science is recognised as a complex multidisciplinary subject ranging from computer and telecommunications through cybernetics to psychology, logic and techniques of classification and indexing, and as such the information work and information science may be defined briefly as professional disciplines concerned with the accumulation, storage and transfer of recorded knowledge.

Harrod's Librarians' Glossary defines Information Science as the study of the use of information, its sources and development; usually taken to refer to the role of scientific, industrial, and specialised libraries and information units in the handling and dissemination of information.

Glynn Harmon opines that Information Science evolved not only an expansion or a metamorphosis of documentation and information retrieval, but, also directly or indirectly incorporated or paralled "several prevailing objectives or concepts of the communication and behavioural sciences and other contributory disciplines.

Shera is of the view that librarianship is a generic term and information science is an area of research which draws its substance, methods and techniques from a variety of disciplines to achieve and understanding of the properties, behaviour and flow of information.... Information science contributes to the theoretical and intellectual base for the library operations.

According to Harold Borko, "Information Science is that discipline that investigates the properties and behaviour of information, the forces governing the flow and use of information, and the means of processing information for optimum accessibility and usability. It is concerned with that body of knowledge relating to the origination, collection, organisation, storage, retrieval interpretation, transmission, transformation and utilisation of information. This includes the investigation of information representations in both natural and artificial systems, the use of codes for efficient message, transmission, and the study of information processing devices and techniques such as computers and their programming systems. It is an interdisciplinary science which is derived from and related to such fields as mathematics, logic, lingustics, psychology, computer technology, operations research, the graphic arts, communications, library science, management and other similar fields. It has both a pure science component, which inquires into the subject without regard to its application, and an applied science component, which develops services and products".

INFORMATICS

In Russia and other east European countries, Informatics is used more or less as an equivalent concept to Information Science. It is being used since 1966. The term, informatics is inextricably linked with documents and the information contained in them. According to Harrod's Librarians' Glossary Informatics is: i)the processes, methods and laws relating to the recording, analytical - synthetical processing, storage, retrieval and dissemination of scholarly communication as such which is the attribute of the respective science or discipline; ii)the study of the structure of knowledge and of its embodiment in information handling systems; and iii)the study of the handling and communication of information, particularly by automated and electronic methods.

Informatics is the science of information. It studies the representation, processing and communication of information in natural and artificial systems. Since computers, individuals and organizations all process information, informatics has computational, cognitive and social aspects.

Informatics is the discipline of science, which investigates the structure and properties (not specific content) of scientific information activity, its theory, history, methodology and organization.

The French term informatique, together with various translations informatics (English), informatik (German) and informatica (Italian, Spanish) was coined by Dreyfus, in March 1962, and refers to the application of computer to store and process information. The morphology, information + -ics uses 'the accepted form for names of sciences as conics, linguistics, tactics'. (Oxford English Dictionary 1989); information encompasses both science and practice. Phonologically, informatics combines elements from both 'information' and 'automatic', which strengthens its semantic appeal.

SCOPE OF INFORMATICS

What are the areas common in informatics: the focus on information and how it is represented, processed and communicated between a variety of systems. Representations include paper, analogue and digital records of texts, sounds and images, as well as, for instance, the information represented in a gene and the memories of an individual or an organization.

Informatics studies the interaction of information with individuals and organizations, as well as the fundamental of computation and computability, and the hardware and software technologies used to store, process and communicate digitized information. It includes the study of communication as a process that links people together, to affect the behaviour of individuals and organizations.

INFORMATICS AS A SCIENCE

Science progresses by defining, developing, criticizing and refining new concepts, in order to account for observed phenomena, Informatics is developing its own fundamental concepts of communication, knowledge, data, secrecy, interaction and information, relating them to such phenomena as computation, thought and language and applying them to develop tools for the management of information resources.

Informatics has many aspects. It encompasses, and builds on a number of existing academic disciplines: Primarily, Artificial Intelligence, Cognitive Science and Computer Science. Each takes part of informatics as its natural domain: in broad terms, Cognitive Science concerns the study of natural information processing systems, Computer Science concerns the analysis of computation and design of computing systems; and Artificial Intelligence plays a connecting role, producing systems designed to emulate by, other disciplines, such as Mathematics, Electronics, Biology, Linguistics, Psychology and Sociology. Thus informatics provides a link between disciplines with their own methodologies and perspective, bringing together a common scientific paradigm, common engineering methods and a pervasive stimulus from both technological development and practical application.

Informatics builds on a long tradition of work in logic, which provides an analysis of meaning, proof and truth. It draws on probability and statistics to relate data and information, and on the more recent tradition of computer science for abstract models of computation and fundamental notions of computability and complexity.

The science of information provides a new paradigm of scientific analysis, which concentrates on the processing and communication & information rather than focusing on the electrical, optical, mechanical or chemical interactions that embody this activity. Informatics provides accounts of the representation, processing and communication of information, the conceptual basis for applying computing and information technologies to develop new tools for the management of information in diverse areas, and also the basis for beginning to unravel the working of the mind.

INFORMATION TECHNOLOGY

The two words, information and technology, used together, have acquired special meaning and interpretation during 1990s. It is only recently that the term has been used as a collective term for the whole spectrum of technologies providing the ways and means to acquire, store, transmit, retrieve and process information.

According to the Webster's New Encyclopedia, Information technology is the collective term for the various technologies involved in the processing and transmission of information. They include computing, telecommunication and microelectronics. Whereas Information technology is a development of information sources handled by computers and communicated by electronic channels, databases can thus be accessed by telephone and television links, and computer output can be transmitted in an electronic format directly to a remote receiver.

Rowley opines that "Information technology means the collection, storage, processing, dissemination and use of information. It is not confined to hardware and software, but acknowledges the importance of man and goals he sets for this technology, the values employed in making the choices, the assessment criterion used to decide whether he is controlling and being enriched by it."

UNESCO defines information technology as "scientific, technological and engineering disciplines and the management techniques used in information handling and processing; their applications; computers and their interaction with men and machines; and associated social, economic and cultural matters."

Information technology plays a major role in the management of information. By the application of it the modern technological developments are being exploited to record, process, store, transfer and retrieve the information. An analysis of the aforesaid definitions will reveal that information technology is a combination of technologies such as computer technology, telecommunication systems and services, micrographic and reprographic technology; and information storage technology.

REFERENCES

1. Bhattacharyya,G: Information Science : A unified view through a system approach. Calcutta, IASLIC, 1978.p.18.
2. Bhattacharyya,G: ibid.p.19
3. Borko, H: Information Science: What is it? American Documentation. January, 1968.p.1.
4. Bose,H: Information Science: Principles and practice. New Delhi, Sterling, 1986.p.9.
5. Devarajan,G,Ed: Bibliometric studies. New Delhi, ESS ESS, 1997.p.15-16.
6. Encyclopedia Britanica.ed.15.v.6-Micropedia.Chicago, Encyclopedia Britanica Inc. 1993.p.312.
7. Harrod's Librarians' Glossary and Reference Book.ed.5.USA, Gower pub.Co.1984.p.376.
8. Harrod's Librarians' Glossary of terms used in librarianship documentation, and the book crafts and reference Book. Ed.5.USA, Gower Pub.Co.1984.p.378.
9. Harrod's Librarians' Glossary. ed8. England, Gower, 1995.p.319.
10. Ibid.P.11.

11. Kumar, PSG: Fundamentals of Information Science. New Delhi.S.Chand and Co.,1998.p.13.

12. Kumar,PSG: ibid .p.24.

13. Machlup,F and Mansfield,U: Study of information, interdisciplinary messages. New York, Wiley.1983.p.743.

14. McGarry,KJ: Changing context of information: An introductory analysis.London, Clive Bingly.1981.p.13.

15. Mckee, Bob: Informationstudies.Libr.Ass.Rec.1986.88(5)pp.236-39.

16. Molhot,Pat: The nature of information and its influence on libraries. Special Libraries. July 1984.p.247.

17. Prasher,RG: Information and communication. ILA Bulletin 23(3)1987.p.18.

18. Random House Dictionary of English Language. New York, Random House,1966

19. Rojas,B A: Information systems for the Scientific Management of Agfricultural Research - Conference on selected issues of Agricultural Research in Latin America. Madrid,1982.ISNAR.March, 19814.

20. Rowley, Jennifer E: The basics of information technology. London, Clive Bingly, 1988.p.1.

21. Sathyanarayana,R: Information Technology and its facets. New Delhi, Manak,1996.p.8.

22. Shera,JH: The foundation of education for librarianship. New York, Becker & Hayes, 1972.

23. The Oxford English Dictionary. Ed2.v.8. Oxford, Clarenden Press, 1989.p.944.

24. The World Bank: World Development report: Knowledge for Development, 1998-99 New York, OUP Press.p.1.

25. UNESCO: World information report, 1997-98.Paris, UNESCO.pp.271-72.

26. Van Nostrand's Scientific Encyclopeadia. Ed.8.New York, Van Nostrand's and Reinhold.1994.p.1701.

27. Webster's New Encyclopedia. New York, Printice Hall, 1992.p.565.

28. William, William F: Principles of automated information retrieval. Illinois, Business press, 1965.

29. Zorkoczy,P and Heap, N: Information Technology. ed. 4. London, Pitman. 1995. p. 7.

Chapter 2

Information and Knowledge Management in the I.T. Environment

INTRODUCTION

Information, a self-regenerative resource, is a socio-economic product. Academicians, R & D personnel, planners, policy makers etc realize that it is an important resource for their day to day activities. It is an instrument of social change, a non-depleting resource, a commodity subject to economic analysis.

The beginning of the 21st century appears to be ushering a new era of human life with a number of very significant inexorable changes at a rapid speed. The changes are caused by the following.

i) Information as Primary Superpower

Information today is deemed to be the primary superpower that supplies energies to deal with all human developments and growth and also to combat every negative force that threatens the very human existence. Governments of all countries, industries and business houses and other organizations are heavily investing in the production and growth of new knowledge than ever before to be in the forefront of economic and political spheres and save human society from disasters.

ii) Information and Communication Technology

The technology in general, more precisely, information and communication technology is the chief enabling agent of changes, at the same time the cause for many of these changes.

iii) Digital Technology

Digital technology that is being widely applied to all process of information storage, retrieval and communication, said to be sweeping the world currently, is the focus of attention, Indian Economy and Information.

In this context it is noteworthy that the Indian economy, presently, is poised for an unprecedented accelerated economic growth. The economic schools of thought are predicting that the country could leapfrog to become an economic power in the next few decades. Another notable point is, demographically India will have the youngest workforce of any large economy, status that will be maintained for long. India will be the largest contributor to the additional work force and population globally over the next few decades. Converting the growing working population into a virtuous asset, creative productive jobs, higher consumption, higher savings, higher investments leading to higher levels of economic growth represent the greatest promise and severe challenges to respond. While the promise of economic prosperity comforts us, there are also forces that could retard progress and pull the economy backwards.

Despite these strength and weaknesses the Government of India has launched the National knowledge Commission to harness our strength effectively and also combat our weaknesses, by creating a knowledge base and build up the necessary human capital. The National Knowledge commission envisages five significant aspects such as knowledge concepts, access to knowledge, knowledge creation, knowledge application and knowledge services. It has given a very strategic role to libraries and information centers to provide all the information and knowledge support to the process of economic development and growth.

INFORMATION MANAGEMENT

Societies' focus on information and knowledge gave rise to a new discipline called Information Management (IM). In the words of Peter Vickers the concept of information management can be viewed as:

i) Management of information is not concerned simply with documents, messages;

ii) Information has to be treated as a resource. It requires proper management like money, manpower and materials;

iii) At the simplest level, IM involves planning and coordination of

- Information handling skills,
- Information technology ; and
- Information sources and services'

iv) IM requires a careful watch on the new developments that can contribute to the better management of information sources;

v) IM requires an understanding of pattern of information flow within the organization, and thus it demands a systematic mapping and monitoring of such flows.

According to Linda Woodman information management is everything referring to obtaining the adequate information, in adequate way, for the adequate person, at an adequate cost, in the adequate time and place, to take the adequate decision. In fact information management encompasses

- People
- Process
- Technology
- Content

FACETS OF INFORMATION MANAGEMENT

There are five facets of Information Management

- External information
  - Information Resource Management (IRM)
  - Information technology (IT)
- Internal Information
  - Management Information System (MIS)
  - Information System (IS)
- Converting
  - Information technology
  - Information processing
- Actionable knowledge
  - Strategic information management
- Cost-effective manner
  - Strategic information management
  - Information resource management

The aforesaid components are based on six activities. Therefore, information management is a combination of the following disciplines:

- Information Technology (IT);
- Management Information system (MIS);
- Strategic Information system;
- Information Resource Management System (IRM);
- Information Processing; and
- Information Systems.

INFORMATION TECHNOLOGY (IT)

IT is a technology of technologies. It includes acquisition, processing, storage and dissemination of vocal, pictorial ,textual and numerical information by a microelectronics-based combination of computing and telecommunications. Information technology has arisen as a separate technology by the convergence of data processing techniques and telecommunications, the former providing the capabilities for processing and storing information and the latter the vehicle for communicating it. Advances in telecommunication have made it possible to transfer information from any place to any parts of the globe at extremely high speed. Online access of distant databases is made possible instantaneously. Electronic document processing and delivery are the gifts of information technology. Development of expert systems can be applied to information and documentation tasks enriching retrieval function. Internet technology, an offshoot of IT has made the information services highly cost-effective. In fact, development of hypertext and hypermedia have made searching very simple. The structured approach to information seeking is no longer required. These achievements have made IT a strong tool of IM.

MANAGEMENT INFORMATION SYSTEM (MIS)

MIS is a system designed to provide management and supervisory information with required data that is accurate, relevant and timely, possibly on a real time basis. This type of information is necessary for decision making. In fact, MIS is an integrated computerized system, covering both internal and external information for management and decision - making, in a given organization.

STRATEGIC INFORMATION MANAGEMENT

Strategy includes all the management functions such as planning, staffing, control, marketing, reporting, finance, production, evaluation etc. The strategic information connotes information which supports strategy. Information is general, is a strategic resource of any organization. This means, information is not merely to be used, it is to be used to meet the strategic goals of an organization by improving the performance. Strategic information management provides the purpose for information management.

INFORMATION RESOURCE MANAGEMENT (IRM)

Information Resource Management deals with applying management techniques such as planning, evaluation, control etc and treating information as a resource like men, material, machine and money. In general sense it implies the management of all resources of an organization itself.

INFORMATION PROCESSING

Information processing is a complex set of activities where data is modified into a more useful form. After modification, it may be an information or may still remain just refined data, depending on how it is expected to be used. Information processing helps in decision making. A set of data is processed and an output is generated. This processing is based on some assumption, principles and knowledge in a specific field. Processing is done on the basis of logic, intelligence, experience and knowledge.

INFORMATION SYSTEM

Information system is a set of arrangement of things so related or connected to form a unity or organization. It comprises of the documentation centers and the communication systems. Information systems deal with the current status of the organization. Its business functions, data requirements, data sources, potential opportunities, evaluation, priorities organizational structure, control mechanism, etc.

IMPLEMENTATION OF IM

When IM is to be implemented one must view the components of IM as process of activities. A number of models are available for IM. UK's Stanford Life Assurance Model proposed by Chester Simpson has the following steps.

i) Formulate the problem;

ii) Identify information needs;

iii) Locate/capture appropriate information;

iv) Analyse/interpret it;

v) Manipulate/package it;

vi) Distribute it;

vii) Store and dispose of it; and

viii) Use it.

IBM's Market Information Capture process proposed by Thomas Davenport has the following steps.

- Requirements managements;
- Information asset plan;
- Information systems plan;
- Acquisition;
- Analysis;
- Dissemination; and
- Feedback.

IMPLEMENTATION TECHNIQUES

The implementation techniques include i) Understanding Information environment, ii) Information audit, iii) Information mapping and mining, and iv) Content management.

INFORMATION ENVIRONMENT

Understanding the information environment is the first step towards implementing information management. Information environment has a very significant role to play in information management. This is because of the following reasons.

- Information management is not something which can be implemented once and be done away with. It is not a one time activity. It is an ongoing process.
- When information management is implemented with a thorough knowledge of information environment, it will have to incorporate the organisation's vision.
- Study of information management provides a holistic approach to information management.
- Study of information environment makes information management more human- centred than machine-

centred.

- When information management is based on the study of environment in which it is expected to be applied, it is more practical.

INFORMATION AUDIT

Information audit is the next logical step towards implementation of information management. It is a systematic process through which an organization can understand its information needs, what it knows, information flows and gaps. In other words information audit deals with what information is required and how it is used. In this context, information can be considered as an object or a resource in a document. It can also be viewed as a product of human thinking, human behavior and social process. Information audit constitutes three important components such as i) information need; ii) information acquisition; and iii) information use.

INFORMATION MAPPING AND MINING

The next step towards information management is to procure and store information in such a manner that it can be accessed and used for decision making in different situations. Such a mechanism of storing and facilitating the use of information or knowledge is the essence of information mapping and mining. Information mapping is based on the patterns of expectations or information needs of human brain from an information resource. It gives a systematic framework to the information content. While data mining is a technological device aiming at interpreting and transforming the docile and sometimes dead data into live and useable information or knowledge.

CONTENT MANAGEMENT

Content management is effectively collecting, managing and making information available in targeted publication. Content management is viewed in the context of the web sites or web-based information resources. It is relevant in the area of web-based information.

INFORMATION MANAGEMENT - CHALLENGES

Organisations are confronted with many information management problems. In many ways, the growth of electronic information has only worsened these issues over the last decade. Common information management problems include:

- Large number of disparate information management systems;
- Little integration or coordination between information systems;
- Range of legacy systems requiring upgrading or replacement;
- Direct competition between information management systems;
- No clear strategic direction for the overall technology environment;
- Limited and patchy adoption of existing information systems by staff;
- Poor quality of information, including lack of consistency, duplication, and out of date information;
- Little recognition and support of information management by senior management;
- Limited resources for deploying, managing or improving information systems;

- Lack of enterprise-wide definitions for information types and values;
- Large number of diverse business needs and issues to be addressed; Lack of clarity around broader organizational strategies and directions;
- Difficulties in changing working practices and process of staff; and
- Internal politics impacting on the ability to coordinate activities enterprise-wide.

KNOWLEDGE MANAGEMENT IN LIBRARIES

The conventional functions of a library are to collect, process, disseminate, store and utilize document information to provide service for the society. In the knowledge economy era the library will become an important link in the knowledge innovation chain. In the 21st century, the library will inevitably face the new subject of knowledge management. Knowledge management requires linkage of information with information, information with activities and information with man - so as to realize the sharing of knowledge including explicit and tacit knowledge.

According to Wang Yunhua, in the knowledge economy era, the management refers to effectively identify, acquire, develop, resolve, use store and share knowledge, to create an approach to transforming and sharing of the tacit and explicit knowledge and to raise the emergency and innovation capability by utilizing the wisdom of the team. Since knowledge has become the driving force for social development, the attention of the society to information and knowledge is rising and people's demands for information and knowledge are increasing step by step. This has provided a good environment for library development. Moreover, as information and knowledge have become important productive factors for the modern economic system, the society will inevitably require intensified management of information and knowledge. How to manage knowledge will become an important subject facing libraries in the near future. Knowledge management in libraries should be focused on effective research and development of knowledge, creation of knowledge bases, exchange and sharing of knowledge between library staffs, training of library staff, speeding up explicit processing of the implicit knowledge and realizing of its sharing.

CHARACTERISTICS OF KNOWLEDGE MANAGEMENT

The role of Knowledge management in libraries will become more and more important along with the development of knowledge economy. The significant characteristics are the following:

Human Resource Management

It is the core knowledge management in libraries. The most important resource in the knowledge economy system is the talents who grasp knowledge. The libraries will attach importance to vocational training and lifelong education of library staffs to raise their scientific knowledge level and ability of acquiring and innovating knowledge.

Promote Knowledge Innovation

i) Knowledge innovation is the core of the knowledge economy society. For collection, processing, storage and dissemination of knowledge and information, libraries represent an indispensable link in the scientific system chain, an important link in the knowledge innovation.

ii) The library work is a component of knowledge innovation;

iii) Libraries must pay attention to diffusion and conversion of knowledge;

iv) Knowledge management in libraries is to promote relationship in and between libraries, between library and user, to strengthen knowledge internet working and to quicken knowledge flow; and

v) In the knowledge economy era, libraries will carry out researches on development and application of information resources, construction of virtual libraries, protection of intellectual property rights in the electronic era etc thus founding the base for knowledge innovation.

Information Technology

Information technology is a tool for knowledge management in libraries. Knowledge acquisition is the starting point of knowledge management in libraries. The application of information technologies enlarges the scope of knowledge acquisition speed and reduces knowledge acquisition cost. It is impossible to accomplish such important tasks by using man's brains only in the modern society in which the knowledge changes with each passing day. It will be possible to link closely knowledge sources and knowledge workers by computer networks, thus constructing knowledge networks in libraries based on realization of single point information (Wang Delu).

CONTENTS OF KNOWLEDGE MANAGEMENT IN LIBRARIES

The knowledge management in libraries constitutes the following:

Knowledge Innovation Management

It includes three aspects viz theoretical innovation management of knowledge, technical innovation management and organizational innovation management.

Theoretical innovation management is to enrich and enlarge the theoretical and practical research fields in Library and Information Science. Technical innovation management is to manage the network systems constructed by the organizations. Organisational innovation management is to create a set of effective organizational management systems adaptable to the requirements in the electronic library.

Knowledge Dissemination Management

Libraries may play the part of knowledge tosser, use diverse media and channels to disseminate various new knowledge. In the 21st century, the Internet, with its mass information and extensive contents, will provide people with the main approach to searching knowledge and acquiring information.

Knowledge Application Management

In the 21st century libraries should also attach importance to provision of services for users to acquire knowledge and achieve maximum functions and efficiency of knowledge information.

Therefore, knowledge services based on high-speed information networks should be attempted by the following.

i) Setting up virtual libraries for enterprises, governments, public organizations and Scientific and R & D institutions.

ii) Setting up digitized knowledge services which is actually a development trend of libraries in the 21st century.

iii) Digitise libraries resources. The knowledge services of libraries in the future will start with databases comprising electronic journals and books in different languages can operate on high speed information networks. Great efforts should be made to transform all existing large non-electronic information resources into electronic information and integrate them into electronic libraries.

iv) Setting up of library web portal and institutional repositories as part of dissemination of information and knowledge services.

CONCLUSION

Knowledge management has become a powerful tool for promoting innovation and realizing reengineering the various walks of life. It occupies a very outstanding position in the creation of the knowledge innovation systems of a country. How far the library circles to meet the challenge of knowledge economy and to build the knowledge management system of libraries is a subject that demands our urgent attention.

REFERENCES

1. Ackoff, RL: Towards a behavioural theory of communication. Management Science.4.pp.218-34.

2. Corbin, Lisa: Speeding up the data: Superhighway. Observer.31January,1996

3. Davenport, Thomas: Information ecology: Mastering the Information and knowledge environment. New York, OUP,1997.

4. Ganesh Natarajan and Sandhya Shkhar. Knowledge management: Enabling business growth. New Delhi, McGraw Hill , 2000.

5. Kamalavijayan, D: Information and knowledge management. Delhi, Macmillan India, 2005

6. Martin, William: The global information society. London, Aslib, 1995.

7. Prytherch, Ray: Information Management and Library Science: A guide to the literature. Aldershot, Gower, 1994.

8. Yovits, MC: Information Science: Towards the development of a true scientific discipline. American Documentation. 20, 1969.

Chapter 3

Information Literacy in the Digital World

Giving a stunning vision of future, Alvin Toffler discusses in Power Shift about force, wealth and knowledge, the three sources of power. Information or knowledge is gaining importance over other sources of power with every fleeting nano second. The advanced economy cannot run without information systems and knowledge of the new complexities of production and integration of diverse and constantly changing technologies. Knowledge therefore is not only the dominant of the three sources of power, but the most important constituent of the other two sources, force and wealth. Toffler points out the power shift is the hidden shift of the relationship between force, wealth and knowledge. It is an accepted fact that information or knowledge will rule the 21st century. In this context information literacy programmes can be considered means of effective use of I.T enabled information and knowledge-embedded information systems and services in the knowledge society.

The concept of Information literacy is the ability to recognise when information is needed, to identify, locate, evaluate, organise, and effectively create, use and communicate information from a variety of sources. To be an information literate, a person must be able to recognise when information is needed and must have the ability to locate, evaluate and use effectively the needed information. A literate person is one who

- recognises the need for information;
- recognises that accurate and complete information is the basis for intelligent decision making;
- identifies potential sources of information;
- develops successful search strategies;
- accesses sources of information, including computer-based and other technologies ;
- evaluates information;
- organises information for practical application;
- integrates new information into an existing body of knowledge; and
- uses information in critical thinking and problem solving.

The greatest challenge for society in the 21st century is keeping pace with the knowledge and technological expertise necessary for finding, applying and evaluating information. Given in the ever-expanding sea of information at our disposal, analysis of an information need, knowledge of resource types, evaluation of access tools, and interpretation of results are critical to successful information retrieval.

WHY INFORMATION LITERACY?

There are a number of factors which warrants information literacy skills in the 21st century such as:

- abundant information choices;

- effective use of information resources;
- availability of number of channels like libraries, community resources, mass media, internet, special internet groups;
- effective use of ICT tools and digital sources;
- unfiltered information raising questions of validity, reliability and authenticity;
- the existence of information in multiple media which requires ability to handle etc.

FACETS OF INFORMATION LITERACY

The facets of information literacy include visual literacy, media literacy, computer literacy, digital literacy and network literacy. Information literacy is the integration of all these different literacies. Through information literacy other literacies can be achieved.

Condorcet and Shapiro opine that "information literacy education is essential to the future democracy, if citizens are to be intelligent shapers of the information society rather than pawns, and to humanistic culture, if information is to be part of a meaningful existence rather than a routine of production and consumption. They have suggested seven important components of holistic approach to information literacy such as:

- Tool literacy or the ability to understand and use the practical and conceptual tools of current information technology relevant to education;
- Resource literacy or the ability to understand the form, format, location and access methods of information resources;
- Social-Structural literacy or understanding how

information is socially situated and produced;

- Research literacy or the ability to understand and use the I.T based tools relevant to the research scholar;
- Publishing literacy or the ability to format and publish research and ideas electronically;
- Emerging technology literacy or the ability to continuously adapt to, understand, evaluate and make use of the continually emerging innovations in the IT;
- Critical literacy or the ability to evaluate critically the intellectual human and social strengths and weaknesses, potentials and limits, benefits and costs of IT."

INFORMATION LITERACY AND EDUCATION

Information literacy is important to higher education, as it is a part of and contributor to, life long learning. At the same time, developing lifelong learners is the central mission of higher education institutions. If individuals are able to think critically, and learn, they need the help of these institutions. Colleges and universities provide the foundation to continue to grow intellectually throughout their careers, and such individuals contribute to society as informed citizens. Information literacy provides these individuals with the tools to do so.

Information literacy helps the individual to extend learning beyond the formal class room settings. It provides practice with self directed investigations. These lead individuals to attain best professional positions and to shoulder increasing responsibilities in arenas of life. Thus information literacy augments students' competency with evaluating, managing and using information.

One successful method for developing information

literacy skills is through resource based leaning or library centred learning. This involves student's assuming more responsibility for locating materials, from which to learn. This also develops life long learning skills.

An information literate student can determine the nature and extent of the information required. He can effectively and efficiently access to that information and its sources critically and make use of the selected information for a specific purpose. He can also understand the economic, legal and social issues regarding access and use of the information.

The inclusion of information competencies as a graduation requirement is the key that will fully integrate information literacy into the curricula of academic institutions. Information literacy instruction in higher education can take a variety of forms such as stand alone course or classes, on-line tutorials, workbooks, courses related instruction or course integrated instruction. State-wide university systems and individual colleges and universities can undertake strategic planning to determine information competencies, to incorporate instruction in information competence throughout the curriculum and to add information competence as a graduation requirement for students.

INFORMATION LITERACY IN LIBRARIES

Libraries have centrally positioned themselves in defining and implementing information literacy programmes, because, libraries are intimately concerned with information. The contemporary library is not simply a repository for information but a dynamic gateway to information. The library's changing role from repository to gateway came with the advent of information and communication technology would become an integral part of all libraries providing greater efficiencies for both librarians and users.

Information literacy necessitates positive change in the instructional mission of library. The library's expanded instructional role emphasises information seeking behaviour within the context of an information need. Today's library instruction is focused on teaching students research strategies that require active engagement, fosters problem solving and its emphasis is on enabling students to become independent researchers and on encouraging lifelong learning.

Information literacy requires an awareness of the way in which information systems work, of the dynamic link between a particular information need and sources and channels required to satisfy that need. Information literacy is being considered as new paradigms in library services.

College libraries have an important role in improving the quality of undergraduate education. The role of college libraries has changed, beyond collecting, organising and preserving materials, with the development of information literacy programmes in education. They can improve the quality by participating in and strengthening information literacy programmes. These libraries can actively involve themselves in all aspects of higher education, teaching, research and publications, At the same time, they can create climate which encourages lifelong learning, and can instruct students, faculty and staff.

Librarians can also involve themselves with the educational process as they actively participate in debate in undergraduate education. The librarians have the talents and skills in library instruction and they are partner to, or collaborator with Information teaching faculty.

LITERACY AND INFORMATION TECHNOLOGY

Information Literacy is related to information technique skills. Information technology skill enables an individual to use computers, software applications, databases and other technologies to achieve a wide variety of academic and personal goals. Information literate individuals should necessarily develop some ICT skills. Technology is changing the way higher educational institutions are offering instruction. The use of the internet is being taught in the contexts of subject area curricula and the overall information literacy process. There is some empirical indication that students who use technology as a tool may become better at managing information, communicating, and presenting ideas. Digital divide is chiefly responsible for information illiteracy in digital environment.

CONCLUSION

The rapidly evolving information landscape means that education methods and practices must evolve and adapt accordingly. Information must become a key focus of educational institutions at all levels. This requires a commitment of students to life long learning and an ability to seek out and identify innovations that will be needed to keep pace with or outpace with changes, educational methods and practices, within our increasingly information-centric society. Information literacy must facilitate and enhance a student's ability to harness the power of information. Key to harnessing the power of information is the ability to evaluate information, to ascertain its relevance, authenticity and modernity. Critical thinking is an important educational outcome for students. Education institutions should formulate strategies to help for critical thinking, as a means to enhance information evaluation and information literacy among students. Information literacy will help teachers acquire the information competency skills necessary to locate information needs for their curricular and extra-curricular needs so as to make them life-long learners and impart these skills to their students wherever necessary. Our teachers and students in future should have problem - solving, imaginative and creative thinking skills as they access information and create nascent knowledge. A vibrant educated information literate society is needed rather than a society of educated information illiterates. Information literacy will pave way for information empowerment to compete in the knowledge society.

REFERENCES

1. Andretta, Susie and Cutting, Andrew: Information literacy: A plug- and-play approach.Libri.53(3)2003.pp202-209.
2. Homann, B: Difficulties and new approaches in user education in Germany .The Hague, IFLA,2001.
3. Koch, M: Information Literacy: Where do we go from here? Techno quarterly for Education and Technolgy.10(1) 2003.
4. Pejova, Z: Information literacy: An issue which requests urgent action in developing countries and countries in transition. Prague, UNESCO,2003.
5. Rader HB: Information literacy: An emerging global priority, Prague, UNESCO, 2002.
6. Whitehead, MJ and Quilan, CA: Canada: An information literacy case study. Prague, UNESCO, 2002.

Chapter 4

Sociology of Information Services

INTRODUCTION

Information is an important resource and vital input for socio-economic and cultural development of a nation. The globalization of Information flows is in intensifying competition, raising the danger that the poorest countries and communities will fall behind more rapidly than ever before. Today, even developing countries like India speak more and more about cyberspace and information superhighway. But, third world countries like India should not forget the real situation prevailing in our villages and slums. Many villages are still without electricity, telephone, primary schools and even without primary facility like safe drinking water and sanitation. For the poor the promise of the Information age 'knowledge for all' can still be as remote as a distant star. To bring the promise of Information age close to reality the implications of the Information revolution must be thought of in the proper perspective in the development programmes of developing countries like India.

INFORMATION AS A SOURCE OF SOCIETAL DEVELOPMENT

Information is an essential component of growth and

improvement in living standard. In modern society, information is closely interrelated with growth and development which is reflected in the areas of economic, political, social, occupational and cultural spheres. A sea change is taking place in society due to the application of information and knowledge for development. Information technology with all its spectacular advances has been the chief instrument of these revolutionary changes leading societies to its third phase of development known as 'Information age'. Libraries and information centers should their activities in such a way as to meet the new challenges and fast and sweeping changes taking place in the society.

A number of factors are attributed for the value of information in the present day society. They are mainly research and development, fusion of science and technology, societal, information, information technology and information demand. There are a number of catalytic pressures such as growth of population, social differentiation and reorganization, technological innovation, growth in education, life expectancy increases, social welfare provision etc which have brought forth many demands for information. Today information has become a source of economic and political power and driving force for acquisition of wealth and political strength. In fact, information-rich countries of today are becoming more and more richer and powerful than before on account of expertise in creating new knowledge and information and its effective and efficient utilization. But the poor countries and poor people cannot compete with rich ones not only because they have less capital but because they have less knowledge. Knowledge is often costly to create, and that is why much of it is created in industrial countries.

STRUCTURE OF INDIAN SOCIETY

India is a democratic and secular country with a population of more than 107 crores. Nearly three fourth of the people are living in villages and occupation of the majority is in the field of agriculture. About half of population is illiterate which constitutes half of the total illiterate at the global level. The GNP is low (Us$278.7bn). Quite a good percentage of people are living below poverty line. Unemployment among the educated is high and superstitious belief, child labour and atrocity towards women and children are still prevalent especially in the weaker sections of the society. With all these adverse situations for prospective development India is moving towards the 21st century. Is it possible for such a nation to develop at the desired level it ought to be? In India, the majority are village populace.

The village is the basic unit of social, economic and cultural life of the Indian society. It is also a centre of political and administrative activity. Rural India which has continued to remain neglected for centuries together has now come to be recognized for its immense economic potential. Economists, policy makers, planners and government have come to the conclusion that no socio-economic development can be achieved unless rural masses are fully involved in the programmes and process of economic development. This ultimately led to the ideas of people's participatory planning. Thus the village is now the unit for grass root level planning as envisaged by Gandhiji as Panchayat Raj. People's participatory planning denotes the involvement of the people from the stage of initiation to the completion of the plan. It consists of people's participation in decision making, implementation of decisions, sharing of benefits and evaluation and monitoring of plan. In such a society there would be genuine participation of people in the decision making process in all levels of government. In people-centered development, objectives like improvement of health, education, housing, safe drinking water and social welfare assume paramount significance. For the proper implementation of all these, information input is required by the community. The information requirement of people in one village is different from another village depending upon various social setups. Hence it is imperative to chanalize the need-based information for a multidimensional social development of the country as a whole.

INFORMATION NEEDS OF THE SOCIETY

For an overall development of a society, information input becomes imperative especially in the present day information environment. Local libraries and Information centers under the local Governmental bodies have a crucial role to play in this regard. As rightly observed by B.S.Kesavan the library is no longer a passive institution, but a dynamic institution and it has become an integral part of the society. This concept has changed the nature of the library architecture. Library is now a place where one is completely at home, where the entire family comes along with the *laughter* of children for the enjoyment of life. Unless the libraries are built in beautiful surroundings, they can't perform effective service in the matter attracting readers to activate their minds.

A rural library is a rural information centre which should respond to the need of the community it serves. It has been rightly observed by Bloss that "the conviction is that when people know the facts, they are more apt to make a better life for themselves and to easier to leave with what they don't. A skillfully selected and usefully organized collection of books is a source of ideas for rational action and for improved living. Such a collection can become an active force for good in the community when aggressively and imaginatively exploited".

As a service centre a village library should ascertain the nature of information, need-based, efficient and effective information service. Information need may be in the area of agriculture, industry, education, health, employment, developmental programmes of the Government for the uplift of the down trodden and weaker section of the society etc. The information needs should be ascertained through community survey by local libraries. Based on this baseline data information should be collected from various agencies and information sources and disseminated to the people in the society. Hence attempts should be made at the local level with the initiative of the local government for the establishment of rural information centers (RIC) as an extension of local libraries for the supply of information and for the development of rural community.

RURAL INFORMATION CENTRES IN KERALA

Attempts were made in Kerala for the establishment of rural information centres viz "Sevana" by the Kerala State Library Council in fourteen districts in Kerala on an experimental basis. These are in addition to the district information centres established by the Government at the District head quarters. The services of these centres cannot always be utilized by the rural community due to the distance between the centres and the villages. Considering this aspect Kerala State Library Council launched the programmes of rural information centres. The structure, objective and function of these centres are given below.

As part of the First phase of the programme 14 rural libraries were selected by the State Library Council to function as the rural information centres and as extension to these libraries. In the selection of these libraries preferences were given to libraries which are situated in places where the weaker section of the society live and that are functioning effectively in the region. For the functioning of each centre an annual grant of Rs.5000/- is given by the council. The centre is controlled by an advisory body and services are rendered by the Librarian/Information Assistant. The person who is in charge of the centre has been given necessary training in the collection, organization and dissemination of information. The Kerala State Library Council(KSLC) is the focal point in the collection of information generated at the State level in the field of agriculture, industry, education, health, employment and other developmental programmes for the weaker section of the society announced by the government form time to time etc. The information collected will be routed to the various local information centres in the State by the KSLC.

The sphere of activities or services of the centres include the following:

i) To disseminate information that are useful to the rural community and which are generated by the various departments of the government.

ii) To disseminate information pertaining to education and labour to the rural community.

iii) To provide information pertaining to the welfare programmes intended for the weaker section of the society announced by the government from time to time.

iv) To conduct seminars, conferences and workshops on various subjects such as agriculture, animal husbandry, fishery, public health, industries etc.

v) To prepare students in the rural areas for attending competitive examinations conducted by the State Government and Central Government.

vi) To provide publicity among the rural community regarding the welfare programmes of the government.

vii) To ensure public participation in the developmental programmes at the village level etc.

The establishment of rural information centers in Kerala is a pioneer attempt. The activities of these centres are so much linked with information support to people's participatory planning for grass root level development in Kerala which is recently launched and is a model to other states in Indian Union. According to Prof.Neelameghan there are three distinct but interrelated aspects to be taken note of in considering information support to grass root level development of rural communities . They are:

- Provision for and communication of pertinent data and information to support rural people's efforts for their own development in agriculture, literacy, health, housing, employment, natural resources conservation or environment matters.
- Rural people possess a fund of valuable native knowledge in the areas - food, health and medicine related plants and animals, social and cultural value systems, ethnic, music and arts etc. which need to be recorded, processed, disseminated and utilized on a much wider scale. A good part of such information may not be in written or printed form but transmitted orally.
- Information required for preparing development plans at the national and sub national levels-data on demographic aspects, agriculture and other economic activities, human settlement, health and family welfare etc.is to be provided to the planners, plan implementers and managers and supporting agencies.

In order that the rural information centers function as

true instruments for planning at the local level the activities of the centers should be strengthened. For this, each village should establish a rural information centre as the pivot of information generating centre and support the role of local development of state and thereby country as a whole. The Kerala State Library Council should take up a leading role in this regard and show this as a model to other States in India.

CONCLUSIONS

The significance of information for rural development need not be emphasized. Information condusive to local situation should be provided to the populace on important rural issues in the field of agriculture, industry, education, employment, health and sanitation etc. The local government should identify and establish the rural information centres as vital element in the promotion of socio-economic and cultural development of the society. In the present day information environment a network of rural information centres, with district and national information centres becomes necessary for overall development of the country. The future of 21st century will highly depend on information know-how and those countries which are able to collect, organize and utilize the information effectively and efficiently are going to rule the world. Third world countries like India should bestow more attention on rural development. For this, information access at the local level is imperative for grass root level planning and sustainable societal development.

REFERENCES

1. Bloss, Meredith: Responding to manifest needs. Library Journal.89(16)1964
2. Neelameghan,A: Information technology and rural development.4(1)1988.pp.55-61

3. Sarada.K: Rural library services in India. New Delhi, ESS ESS, 1986.

4. Sharma, Pandey S.K: Libraries and Society. New Delhi, ESS ESS. 1992.

5. Sathyanarayana.M: Public library and community analysis. New Delhi, Reliance Publishing House, 1997.

6. UNESCO: World Information Report. Paris, UNESCO,1998.

Chapter 5

Socio-Economic Factors and Reading Interest of Students

INTRODUCTION

Reading is the art of interpreting printed and written words. It is a basic tool of education and one of the powerful and lasting influences in the promotion of one's personal development in particular and social progress in general. Regular and systematic reading sharpens one's intellect, refines his emotions, elevates tastes and provides perspectives and thereby prepares him for an effective participation in the social and political life. It gives a unifying and civilising force tending to unite social groups through the dissemination of common experiences.

Considering the social goal of reading, it is worthwhile to understand the reading habits of students' community. The attempts in the field of reading habits of secondary school students are few. Moreover, sufficient study of the socio-economic factors on the reading habits of students especially of adolescent group in Indian setting is lacking. Another important reason for choosing secondary school students for the study is the important nature of this stage in the educational settings in Kerala. It represents a crucial transition stage educationally and psychologically. It represents a turning point from secondary education to higher education; psychologically it represents the most important adolescent period.

OBJECTIVES

The primary goal of the study is to analyse the impact of socio-economic factors on the reading habits of students in the secondary schools in Kerala. More specifically the study is aimed at the following:

(i) Relation between the socio-economic background and the reading habits of students;

(ii) Variation in the nature of reading habits amongst students hailing from schools situated in urban, semi-urban and rural areas; and

(iii) The degree of variance between socio-economic variables and reading materials.

SAMPLE AND METHODOLOGY

For data collection, primarily questionnaire method was used. In order to corroborate the findings arrived at from the questionnaire, interview method was also used on a selective basis.

Data was collected from 32 schools. 1850 questionnaires were distributed among students in VIIIth, IXth and Xth classes in these schools in an equitable distribution. Out of these 1226 questionnaires duly filled up by the students were collected. Hence 1226 questionnaires stand as the baseline data for analysis and interpretation of the study.

ANALYSIS

The primary data collected through the questionnaire

and interview methods were subjected to a detailed analysis. A correlative study is carried out in order to understand how far the socio-economic factors influence the reading habits of students in the secondary schools in Kottayam, Educational District, Kerala. Different variables such as subject interest, types of reading materials preferred to read etc. were correlated with the socio-economic factors of the students such as sex, place of residence, caste, parents, occupation, income etc. The analysis was carried out under the following heads:

SUBJECT INTEREST VS. SOCIO-ECONOMIC FACTORS

On correlation of variable it is seen that socio-economic factors influence the subject interest among students. The following observations will show how far the socio-economic factors affect the subject interest.

The data show that the region in which students reside has significant impact on their subject interest. Students from the rural areas prefer to read a higher percentage of literature especially novels when compared to students from urban areas. It has also been noted that the percentage is slightly higher than the general pattern of reading interest in science books among students from urban areas. The data show that community varies the subject interest among students. Among SC/ST students the interest for reading literature especially novels is slightly higher when compared to forward community students and backward community students. Sex is another factor which influences the subject interest among students. It is seen that male students read a higher percentage of literature books when compared to girl students. Moreover, the interest for reading Science books is more among male students than girls. Girls read biographical studies more than male students. Father's occupation is another factor which generally affects the reading interest in subjects among students. Among students whose fathers are farmers a higher percentage (71%) are interested in reading literature especially novels. Among students whose fathers are manual labourers (coolies) the percentage of students reading literature especially novels is high when compared to students whose fathers are in occupational groups such as teachers, engineers, doctors etc.

READING STORY BOOKS VS. SOCIO-ECONOMIC FACTORS

It has been seen from the general trend that the detective stories are the type of story books popularly read by the students. But variations are noticed while correlating with socio-economic variables as below.

The data show that there are slight variations in the reading habit of different types of story books and students' place of residence. The interest for reading of comedy stories, students residing in the rural areas show more interest than urban students. Community is another factor which influences even in the reading of types story books. The data show that interest in reading detective stories is comparatively high among backward community students when compared to students from other communities. But forward community students show a relatively high interest in reading comedy stories. Sex is another important factor which influence the reading habit of types of books. The data reveal that boys read more detective stories and pictorial stories, more interest has been shown by girls than boys. As per the data, it would become evident that reading detective stories is more among students from high income group. The fancy for reading detective is less among students from low income group. Interest for reading comedy stories is also comparatively high in low income groups.

MAGAZINE READING VS. SOCIO-ECONOMIC FACTORS

It has been seen that irrespective of the socio-economic factors majority of the students read 'Balarama'. Their second and third preferences are 'Malayala Manorama' and 'Mangalam'. But slight variations are noticed while correlating with socio-economic variables. These observations are given below.

The community to which the students belong plays a vital role in influencing the reading habits. The SC/ST have given their first preference to 'Malayala Manorama' while the first preference for the backward community and forward community students is 'Balarama'. Moreover the SC/ST students are not at all interested in reading English magazines. Of course, the backward community and forward community students have shown only a slight interest in reading English magazines. It is obvious from data that the favourite magazine among girls is 'Balarama' whereas 'Malayala Manorama' is the favourite magazine among boys. In respect of reading of English magazines, the boys have shown more interest than girls.

Parent's income has a direct bearing on the reading habits of their children. This is very true in the case of magazine reading. Buying capacity of parents and their interest for reading have a lot of influence on their children's reading habits. Data show that students from high income group show more interest in reading 'Balarama" whereas the interest for reading 'Malayala Manorama' weekly is more among students of low income groups. The trend in the reading of 'Malayala Manorama" is in a decreasing one from low income group to middle income group to high income group. In respect of the reading of English magazines the above trend is just the reverse i.e. from high income group to middle income group and from middle group to low income group.

It is clear from data that the place of residence of students has influenced the magazine reading habit. 'Balarama' and 'Malayala Manorama' weeklies are popularly read in the rural areas. Reading of English language magazine is very significant among students residing in the urban areas when compared to students residing in the rural areas.

NEWS PAPER READING VS. SOCIO-ECONOMIC FACTORS

It would be very interesting to note what the students read and how various factors influence their choice of newspapers. The observations are given below.

It is clear from the data that sex influences the news paper reading habits of students. The data show that a high percentage of female students prefer to read 'Malayala Manorama' than male students. But in respect of the reading of 'Deepika' boy students show more interest than girl students.

The SC/ST students show a higher percentage of interest when compared to the general trends in reading the daily 'Malayala Manorama'. The percentage of interest in the reading of 'Malayala Manorama' is in a decreasing trend from backward community students to forward community students. In the case of SC/ST students their second choice of news paper is the 'Mangalam'. This is contrary to the general trend in the reading interest of the population under study.

The data show that irrespective of the socio-economic background of the population the daily 'Malayala Manorama is the most favourite among the urban students. In the use of English dailies, the 'Indian Express' is preferred by the urban as well as rural students without much difference. But in the case of 'The Hindu' it is preferred only by students residing in the urban areas.

As the general pattern of interest, the 'Malayala Manorama', is the most favourite news paper among the population under study. This may be due to the fact, that it is a paper published from Kottayam where from the sample is taken for study. However slight variations are noticed among students because of the occupation of their parents. It is observed from the data that 'Malayala Manorama' is the most favourite among students whose fathers are manual labourers. Regarding the second choice of news paper, students whose fathers are farmers prefer to read 'Deepika'. As regards reading of English dailies, an appreciable percentage of students whose fathers are businessmen, government employees etc. read them.

Income is an important variable which influences the news paper reading habit among students. It can be seen from the data that 'Malayala Manorama' is the most favourite news paper among students from low income families. Of course slight variations are observed from the general trend in the news paper reading among middle income and high income groups. Regarding English news paper reading the preferences for 'The Hindu' and 'Indian Express' are in an ascending order from low income groups to middle income groups then to higher income groups. In fact it can be inferred that students belonging to different income levels have varying tastes in the reading of news paper.

READING OF NEWS PAPER COLUMNS VS. SOCIO-ECONOMIC FACTORS

The socio-economic factors even influence students in the reading of the news paper columns. The following would show how far the reading taste varies from the general pattern due to the socio-economic factors. It can be seen from the data that there are variations in the reading interest due to the differences in the place of residence of the students. The sensational news columns attract more students residing in the urban areas. The urban students have shown relatively a higher percentage of interest than rural students in reading sports columns. It is also noted that interest in reading other news paper columns such as advertisement, editorial, cinema etc. varies with place of residence of students.

Table I would show that caste is another factor which influences the reading of various columns in the news papers. It can be seen from the data that the interest for reading sensational news is so predominant among SC/ST students when compared to students from other communities. As regards interest for reading sports and politics columns an ascending trend is noticed from SC/ST to backward communities and then to forward community students.

Table 1 : Reading of News Paper Columns Vs. Caste

Name of New Paper	SC/ST Community	Backward Community	Forward Community	Total
Advertisement	12	25	60	97
	(13.9%)	(8.7%)	(7.1%)	(8%)
Editorial	3	16	103	122
	(3.4%)	(5.5%)	(12.3%)	(10.1%)
Letter to Editor	1	8	5	14
	(1.1%)	(2.7%)	(3.4%)	(5.5%)
Sports Column	21	84	246	351
	(4.6%)	(5.9%)	(4.1%)	(4.6%)
Politics	3	11	72	86
	(3.4%)	(3.8%)	(8.6%)	(7.1%)
Sensational News	42	125	314	481
	(48.8%)	(43.7%)	(37.6%)	(39.8%)

The sex is another variable which influences the reading of various columns in the news papers by students. Regarding the sensational news, female students are more attracted (44.2%) than male students (34.3%). In the reading of sports columns boys show more interest than girls.

LANGUAGE VS. SOCIO-ECONOMIC FACTORS

The general trend in the reading habits of students shows that majority of them prefer to read Malayalam language books. This is due to the fact that Malayalam is the mother tongue of the majority of the population under study. But variations are noticed in the percentages of preferences for reading English books also. These variations from the general trends can be seen from the following observations.

The regions in which students reside is a factor which influences the selection of the language of the books by the students. It is interesting to note that a good number of students in the urban areas prefer to read English language books. This may be because of the existence of English medium schools in the urban areas. But students are not so much attracted in reading books in English language.

The language of the books chosen by the students and the community of the students have a direct relationship. It can be seen that SC/ST students prefer to read Malayalam language books (99.8%). But the interest in reading Malayalam books is in a decreasing trend in the backward community students. As regards reading of books in English language, students from forward community have shown more interest. The choice of English language books is in a decreasing trend among backward and SC/ST community students.

The sex is another factor which influences the reading habits among students. The data shows the female students read more Malayalam books (98.3%) than male students. But in the reading of English language books boys show relatively more interest than girls.

LEISURE TIME ACTIVITIES VS. SOCIO-ECONOMIC FACTORS

It is interesting to note how far socio-economic factors influence even the leisure time activities of students. The following observations are made under this head.

It can be seen from the data that there are variations in the leisure time activities from the general trend. Reading is the most preferred leisure time activity by the population under study. But this percentage of preference is high among students from forward community. Playing is the second preferred leisure time activity by the population. But the level of interest for playing as a leisure time activity is high among SC/ST students. The interest for viewing cinema decreases from SC/ST to upper communities.

The sex is another important variable which influences the leisure time activities of students. The data show that boys spend most of their leisure time for playing whereas the girls spend their time for reading.

Moreover, interest for viewing cinema as a leisure time activity is more among boys whereas viewing television is a leisure time activity among girls.

It can be seen from the data that income is nother factor which affects the leisure time activities of the students. The students from high income families spend more of their leisure time in reading whereas the time spent for reading is relatively less in low income groups. The students from low income group families spend relatively more time for playing when compared to other income groups. The time spent for viewing TV is comparatively less among students from low income groups. This may be because of the non-availability of TV sets in the low income families.

ANALYSIS OF VARIANCE

A two-way analysis of variance is also undertaken here so as to understand the degree of difference between the variables, socio-economic factors and reading materials. Variables which have show very significant differences alone are discussed here.

The two-way analysis of variables viz. story books vs. family income shows that there is a significant variation in the choice of different types of story books by students. It is also found that the difference is significant in the reading of different types of story books by students from various income groups. This will become clear from the following estimation.

Source of Variations	S.S.	D.F.	F-ratio	5% of F-limit
Between rows (between type of story books)	42455.36	6	6.003928	2.66
Between columns (various income group)	32918.97	3	9.310632	3.16
Residual	21213.79	18		

The two-way analysis of variables viz magazine reading vs community shows that there is a significant difference in the choice of magazine by students. The difference is also significant in the case of students belonging to different communities. This is statistically explained as follows:

Source of Variations	S.S.	D.F.	F-ratio	5% of F-limit
Between rows (magazine reading)	97347.52	17	3.332036	2.00
Between columns (between communities)	16910.71	2	4.920004	3.23
Residual	58431.26	34		

The analysis of variables viz magazine reading vs income shows that there is significant variance between magazine reading and family income of students. The degree of variance is estimated as follows:

Source of Variations	S.S.	D.F.	F-ratio	5% of F-limit
Between rows (between magazine)	73010.61	17	4.095529	1.70
Between columns (income levels)	13171.28	3	4.186775	2.68
Residual	53480.72	51		

The aforesaid analysis shows that a number of socio-economic factors influence the reading habits of students in the secondary schools in Kerala. It is also statistically proved that the degree of variance is very significant, especially in variables like income and community, in the choice of reading materials.

FINDINGS AND CONCLUSION

The analysis of the data has given very interesting results. It was found that socio-economic factors have significant influence on the reading habits of the students. The following are the major observations that could be made from the study:

(i) A higher percentage of students from the rural areas prefer to read literature especially novels when compared to students from urban area. Among SC/ST students the interest for reading literature especially novels is slightly higher when compared to forward community students and backward community students. Male students read a higher percentage of literature books when compared to girl students. Among students whose parents are farmers and manual labourers the interest for reading literature especially novel is high when compared to students whose parents belong to other occupational groups.

(ii) The interest for reading detective stories is more among urban students. In the reading of comedy stories students residing in the rural areas show more interest than urban students. The interest for reading detective stories is comparatively high among backward community students when compared to students from other communities. Boys read more detective stories than girls. More students from high income families read detective stories.

(iii) The SC/ST students prefer to read 'Malayala Manorama' weekly while the students from backward community and forward community students prefer to read 'Balarama'. The SC/ST students are not at all interested in reading English magazines. The most favourite magazine among girl students is 'Balarama' whereas 'Malayala Manorama' is the favourite among boys. The students from high income group show more interest in reading 'Balarama' whereas the interest for reading 'Malayala Manorama' weekly is more among students from low income families.

(iv) Female students prefer to read 'Malayala Manorama' daily than male students. In respect of reading of

'Deepika' daily, boys show more interest than girls. The 'Malayala Manorama' is the most favourite among the urban students. As regards English dailies, 'The Indian Express' is preferred by the urban as well as rural students without much difference wheeas 'The Hindu' is preferred only by students residing in the urban areas. The 'Malayala Manorama' is the most favourite newspaper among students of low income groups.

(v) The sensational news columns in newspapers attract more students residing in the urban areas. The urban students have shown relatively a higher percentage of interest than rural students in reading sports columns. Interest for reading sensational news is so predominant among SC/ST students when compared to students from other communities. In the reading of sports columns boys show more interest than girls.

(vi) The students whose fathers are Government employees and businessmen show significant interest in reading English language books. But SC/ST students prefer to read Malayalam language books. Female students prefer to read more Malayalam books than male students.

(vii) Rading is the most preferred leisure time activity by the population under study. But this percentage of preference is high among students from forward community. The most favourite leisure time activity of boys is playing whereas reading is the favourite among girls. The students from high income families spend more of their leisure time in reading whereas the time spent for reading is relatively less among students in low income groups.

A number of socio-economic factors influence the reading habits of students in the secondary schools in Kerala. The degree of variance is very significant especially in variables like income and community in the choice of reading materials.

REFERENCES

1. Anderson, Verna Divkman : "Reading and Young Children", London, Macmillan,1968.
2. Bound, Goy L, et al: "Reading Difficulties their Diaganosis and Connection"' N.J.Prentice Hall,1979.
3. Devarajan G : "Impact of socio-economic Factors on the Reading Habits of Students in the Secondary Schools Students", (ICSSR Project), Trivandrum, University of Kerala,1992.
4. Gopinathan S. : "A Measure of Reading", IE Survey of Reading Interest and Habits, Singapore Institution of Education,1978.
5. Singhal R.P. : "Indian Schools : A study of Teacher Pupil Relation", New Delhi, Vikas,1988.
6. Staiger, Ralph, Ed : "The Teaching of Reading", Paris, UNISCO. 1979.
7. Vasistha K.K. : "Teacher Education in India", New Delhi, Concept,1979.

Chapter 6

Information Technology in Higher Education

INTRODUCTION

The societal development of a nation is highly dependent on the type and quality of education imparted at the various levels. Since education is a specific mode of social practice and a collective endeavour sponsored by the society in a particular set of environments, neither its meaning nor its form can remain the same for a long time. As and when the conditions of our social existence undergo a change, significant shifts in the content and form of education are imperative. A radical transformation in education especially in higher education is called for. This is needed to meet the new challenges in education and thereby to meet the needs of the information society.

The higher education community is planning for a world of which information technology will be so pervasive that the very institution of higher education will change. Of course, IT probably can be used to improve higher education . But IT is exceedingly flexible, and we will face numerous choices about how best to apply it. Some of these choices are straight forward matters of efficiency, best left to technical experts. Other choices will require us to reflect carefully on the values that higher education institutions ought to express. If educators have learned anything from attempts to improve life using IT, it is that significant improvements are possible only when institutions are rethought.

PROBLEMS IN HIGHER EDUCATION

Higher education in India faces a number of problems. These include decline in standard of education, disparities in higher education, unemployment among the educated, increase in the number of students, frustration among teachers and students etc. A number of seminars and conferences conducted on various occasions in India and various commissions on education have repeatedly stressed these issues and provided a number of recommendations to overcome these problems. But we are far from having made any success yet. The present education system faces a number of challenges such as globalisation, privatisation and liberalisation. Any discussion on higher education should take into consideration these perspectives. Information technology can be considered in the context of globalisation of information.

PROGRESS IN INFORMATION TECHNOLOGY

Information technology is the boon of the present century. It is the combination of several technologies and systems. In fact it is the technology of technologies. Today the information generated at the global level is flowing through information super highways. New knowledge would get disseminated at the global level in no time. The promising and diversified possibilities of information technology have reduced the space and time between people, countries and continents. The third industrial revolution fuelled by the combined powers of information technology, is changing not only the way people work but also their perceptions and insights into the world. Society will emerge from the third industrial revolution as a global village. The possibilities of information technology in disseminating information from the generator to the receipient at a faster rate have high relevance in the present day education. The various aspects of education such as learning, teaching and research which need radical changes are amenable to the application of information technology.

APPLICATION OF INFORMATION TECHNOLOGY IN LEARNING

Information Technology can play a crucial role in the effective learning process of students engaged in higher studies. Today a lot of information is generated through printed world and mass media which has resulted in information explosion. As far as developed countries are concerned this is an opportunity because of the help of information technology. Whereas to the third world countries with information technology still in the nebulus state it is a problem. It is estimated that 3000 pages are being printed every minute at the global level. It is also estimated that information generated at the global level during 24 hours a day is enough to compile an encyclopedia of 24 volumes! The growth rate of publications is greater in Science and technology than in the social sciences. The growth of knowledge in S&T was estimated to be doubling every ten years in 1950 and every five years in 1970. Now it is estimated to have reached the stage of doubling every two years or less. The above data will speak of the mass of literature produced in every branches of knowledge. As far as students in the higher education are concerned they meet with a number of problems to make use of the literature available in their fields of study comprehensively, speedily and with precision. But due to the progress in information technology a student of higher education can make use of CD-ROM data bases on-line data bases, INTERNET web pages and Browsers etc for a voyage from sources to sources that are available in any part of the globe, published in his field of study. Hence learning through a variety of information sources is possible with the application of information technology. Inadequacy of information sources will be is no more a problem, if the avenue of IT is properly utilised.

APPLICATION OF INFORMATION TECHNOLOGY IN TEACHING

Information technology has high relevance on the transformation of the traditional, ineffective and age-old teaching methods which persist in our higher educational institutions. Emerging telecommunication network has the potential of effecting desirable changes in the traditional student/teacher interaction in education. Peer to peer electronic communication in the virtual classroom, the role of the instructor as a monitor of self- taught courses, and collaboration of faculty in replaying information to the students are all facilitated by information technology.

Bibliographic instruction through computer assisted instruction packages can be used as effective teaching aids for imparting discipline-wise instruction to students in various subjects like Botany, Zoology, Economics, and Computer Science etc. In fact it is introduction to the user of the information resources available in particular subject disciplines and the techniques of use of those resources.

The distance education programmes can be effectively imparted by using the facilities available in IT. Lecture classes as well as practical classes can be effectively conducted through Television, visual techniques and computer aided instruction packages. Hence students of higher education enrolled either in the formal channel or informal channel will get the services of highly experienced and highly competent teachers from his own country or other countries by the progress of telecommunication.

Multimedia is an important equipment for imparting education to students in higher education. The interactive facility of multimedia can be used to put the user in certain situation in which he will be left to himself to delve deep into the subject. The users can also be supplied with information in visual form that teaches them how to react. Because of the integrated use of several media, it has the capacity to enhance both the comprehension and retention capacity of students.

By making use of various audio-visual equipments for teaching, teaching will become more interesting, effective and fruitful than would be possible through the traditional teaching methods.

APPLICATION OF IT IN RESEARCH

The intelligent use of information tools in transforming higher education requires that there should be changes in the concepts and approaches of present day research. In the National Policy of Education document (section 5.25) it is observed that "in the context of unprecedented explosion of knowledge, higher education has to become dynamic as never before, constantly entering uncharted areas". It may be presumed that globalisation would discourage repetitive research and encourage research workers to become more participative and collaborative with their peer working elsewhere. The application of IT will help in the selection of relevant topics for research, avoid duplication of research, and avoid unnecessary time spent for literature survey. It will facilitate effective data analysis and presentation and dissemination of the research output speedily and effectively, Electronic document delivery service is a boon to the researchers. In fact the progress in IT can be of immense benefit in fruitful and quality research.

The Government, universities and all other concerned

should be aware of the immense possibilities in the application of IT in rejuvenating higher education in India. If we hesitate to imbibe this spirit, we will be lagging far behind in the field of higher education. Hence, increased use of IT in the various fields of higher education for a radical transformation is an educational imperative.

SUGGESTIONS

i) Information is a vital resource and valuable input for societal development of a nation. Hence for the collection, organisation control and effective utilisation of information the Government of India should adopt a National Information Policy.

ii) Radical changes in the traditional teaching methods are to be adopted. Educational media research centers should be established under each university to produce audio and video materials to reinforce and enrich classroom teaching.

iii) For the successful application of IT in higher education, orientation programme should be imparted to students and teachers.

iv) For the supply of professionally qualified manpower in the fields of IT, selected universities in India should start specialised courses in information technology. In this connection it may be noted that the Department of Library and Information Science, University of Kerala had made a maiden attempt by introducing a one year Post-graduate Diploma in Information Technology (PGDIT) in 1996.

v) The academic community in higher education is not satisfied with the present day information services in India. This is mainly due to lack of an academic library/ information system in India. The network system connecting all universities and colleges viz INFLIBNET contemplated by the UGC is of course on the anvil, but the pace of its implementation is slow. Attempts are needed to expedite the implementation of this project as a timebound programme.

CONCLUSION

A document circulated in the world conference on higher education (WCHE) by the UNESCO held in Paris pointed out that the sustainable human development and higher education present a "challenge to us in reconciling economic and social progress with safeguards for the global life support systems".

There are several interrelated factors such as socio-economic, political and cultural factors that are hurdles in the way of application of IT in higher education in India. But we cannot ignore the avenues of IT as pathways for progress of the nation. For revamping education and enhancing its quality and above all for a total quality management (TQM) in higher education it is imperative to utilise the tools and facilities of IT to the maximum possible extent.

REFERENCES

1. Association of Indian Universities(New Delhi). New education policy. New Delhi, AUI,1985.
2. Fitzimmons,J: Information technology and third industrial revolution. Electronic library. 12(5)94p.295-97.
3. Hawkins, BL(199) Distribute learning and institutional restructuring. Educom.Review 34(4)1999.
4. Krishan Kumar: Reference Service.ed.4.New Delhi, Vikas, 1991.p.32.
5. Rajagopalan,T: Some issues in higher education. The Hindu, 9th March.p.22.

Chapter 7
The Digital Divide

INTRODUCTION

Information is a vital and regenerative resource. It is a basic component of societal development. The information and communication technology (ICT) is relied upon heavily by the information centres in order to satisfy the varied information needs of the user community. In all spheares of information activities of mankind there is a significant investment in the Internet as an enterprise and with wide utility to support teaching, scholarship and administrative matters. The application of new technology has accelerated and widened the existing information gap between the rich and poor is growing within a country or even region itself. This leads to "digital divide" between the information "haves" and "have-nots".

The digital divide is the gap between people with effective access to digital and information technology and those with very limited or no access at all. It includes the imbalances in resources and skills needed to effectively participate as a digital citizen. In fact it is the unequal access by some members of society to information and communication technology , and the unequal acquisition of related skills. The term is closely related to the knowledge divide as the lack of technology causes lack of useful information and knowledge.

The term digital divide came into regular usage in the mid 1990s, though the term had previously appeared in several news articles and political speeches as early as 1995. The president of the United States Bill Clinton and his Vice President AlGore used the term in a 1996 speech in Knoxville, Tennessee. There is considerable literature on information and digital inequality that predates this current label. The concept of a digital divide is therefore more a new label than a distinct concept.

DEFINITIONS

There are various definitions of the term 'digital divide'. Digital divide refers to the gap between those who benefit from digital technology and those who do not. Bharat Mehra defines it as 'the troubling gap between those who use computers and the internet and those who do not'. This term initially referred to gaps in the ownership of, or regular access to, a computer. As Internet access came to be seen as a central aspect of computing, the term's usage shifted to encompass gaps not just in the use of computers but also access to the Internet. Recently, some have used the term to refer to gaps in broadband network access. The term can mean not only unequal access to computer hardware, but also inequalities between groups of people in the ability to use information technology fully. Due to the range of criteria which can be used to assess the imbalance, and the lack of detailed data on some aspects of technology usage, the exact nature of the digital divide is both contextual and debatable. Criteria often used to distinguish between the 'haves' and the 'have nots' of the digital divide tend to focus on access to hardware, access to the Internet, and details relating to both categories.

GLOBAL DIGITAL DIVIDE

Another key dimension of the digital divide is the global digital divide, reflecting existing economic divisions in the world. The global digital divide widens the gap in economic divisions around the world. Countries with a wide availability of Internet access can advance the economics of that country on a local and global scale. In today's society, jobs and education are directly related to the Internet, in that the advantages that come from the Internet are so significant that neglecting them would leave a company vulnerable in a changing market. In countries where the Internet and other technologies are not accessible, education is suffering, and uneducated people and societies that are not benefiting from the information age, cannot be competitive in the global economy. This causes to these countries, which tend to be developing countries, to suffer greater economic downfall and richer countries to advance their education and economy. When dealing with the global aspect of digital divide there are several factors such as country of residence, ethnicity , gender, age , educational attainments and income levels etc.

BRIDGING THE DIGITAL DIVIDE

The avenues of information and communication technology have helped in the democratization of information. But more than 80% of people in the world have never even heard a dial tone, let alone surfed the web. In fact the gap between information "haves" and "have-nots" is widening. As far as developing countries are concerned the stratification of information rich and information poor is going to be a big social problem. Various countries and organizations are making attempts to bridge the information gap. Projects like' one laptop per child 'offer a partial solution to the global digital divide. This project tend to rely heavily upon open standards and free open source software. The OLPC XO-1 is an inexpensive laptop computer intended to be distributed to children in developing countries around the world to provide them with access to knowledge. Richard Stallman has highlighted the importance of free software among groups concerned with the digital divide such as the world summit on the information society.

BRIDGING THE DIGITAL DIVIDE-INDIA

National and state-level agencies in India are making attempts to bridge the digital divide. In 2000, the Government of India in collaboration with an information technology started a project, known as the "Hole in the wall" experiment, to provide computer access to the city's street children. An outdoor five-station computer kiosk was set up in one of the poorest slums of New Delhi. Though the computers themselves were inside a booth, the monitors protruded through holes in the walls, as did specially designed joysticks and buttons that substituted for the computer mouse. Keyboards were not provided. The computers were connected to the Internet through dial-up access. A volunteer inside the booth helped to keep the computers and Internet connections running. No teachers or instructors were provided, in line with the concept called 'minimally invasive education'. The idea was to allow the children unfettered 24-hour access, and to learn at their own pace and speed. According to report, children who flocked to the site taught themselves basic computer operations. They worked out how to click and drag objects; select different menus; cut, copy, and paste; get on the Internet; and change the background "wallpaper". A number of projects are being undertaken in various states in India to bridge the Digital divide. The AKSHAYA is a project in Kerala inaugurated by the president of India, Dr.A.P.J.Abdul Kalam on 18th November 2002. The project envisaged the establishment of 9,000 community information centres across the State as part of a campaign to bridge the digital divide. These centres are to be established through private initiative, with the objective of having one centre within two km. of each household. The project would commence in Malappuram and Thiruvananthapuram in January 2003 and the entire state is to be covered by May 2004. As part of the project, one person from each family will be trained to enable him to use the computer for day-to-day communication and information needs.

A shot in the arm for n-Logue is the mandate from the Tamilnadu government to network and put in place the infrastructure required in ten districts. Tamilnadu's Rural Access to services through Internet (RASI) project has already got 70 villages in each of the two districts-Madurai and Cuddalore-networked and are running. And nearly 5-10 villages are getting networked every month in these districts. RASI project seems to be different from other government projects that start with a bang and die even before inaugurations come to an end. It has attracted attention from corporate, educational institutions, hospitals and private telecom companies.

Akin to a PCO booth, the telephone cum Internet access point for a villager will be housed in a kiosk equipped with a PC and CD-ROM and multimedia, web camera, printer, cor DECT wall set, speaker microphone and power backup for four hours. The language barrier has been taken care of by providing local language software. Networking rural India with telephone and the Internet is becoming a reality with "Chiraag".

WHY CLOSING THE DIGITAL DIVIDE MATTERS

Closing the digital divide is a precondition for reducing poverty. Many antipoverty experts believe that closing the digital divide is not a top priority, arguing instead that the poor need clean water and jobs before they need computers. However , what they do not realize is that access to digital technology greatly enhances the effectiveness and affordability of efforts to improve the water supply, improve rural health and education, generate jobs and address any of the other interrelated problems of poverty. Closing the digital divide is not a silver bullet for reducing poverty. But there is a much lower likelihood of large scale and sustainable poverty reduction without doing so.

Closing the digital divide is a precondition for resolving terrorism. Even those who are unconvinced by the antipoverty argument may be convinced by the anti-terrorism argument. It is that the digital divide contributes to terrorism in many ways.

Closing the digital divide is a precondition for achieving world markets. After the dot-com bust in the late 1990s, many came to believe that digital information industries had lost their central role in the world economy. This bust merely showed that technology purchases were slowing in saturated economies. Today, Europe and North America no longer are as dominant in technology as they once were. The emerging market countries of Asia are now major drivers of the digital economy and , in that vast region, the spread of wireless networks is stimulating all other dimensions of economic growth . In fact , the biggest technological growth is occurring outside big cities in these countries. As broadband networks spread into the countryside , costs throughout the supply chain will drop . By adjusting their policies to close the digital divide , the major IT and telecom companies are achieving innovations that could spur growth in the advanced countries as well.

IMPLICATIONS AND ISSUES

Digital divide is marked not only by physical access to computers and connectivity, but also by access to the additional resources that allow people to use technology well in the real sense of the term "digital divide". It gives overriding importance to the physical availability of computers and connectivity, rather than to issues of content, language, education, literacy or community and social resources. A problem with the digital divide concept is its implication on "haves" and "have-nots" but rather a gradation based on different degrees of access to information technology. As Henry Jenkins argues, "the rhetoric of the digital divide holds open this division between civilized tool users and uncivilized non users. As well meaning as it is as a policy initiative, it can be marginalizing and patronizing in its own terms". He also opined that the notion of a digital divide implies a chain of causality i.e. lack of access to computers and the harm being caused by Internet to life chances. While this point is undoubtedly true, the reverse is equally true; those who have already marginalized will have fewer opportunities to access and use computers and the Internet. In fact, technology and society are intertwined and co-constitutive, and this complex in interrelationship makes any assumption of causality problematic. The digital divide framework provides a poor road map for using technology to promote social development since it overemphasizes the importance of the physical presence of computers and connectivity to the exclusion of other factors that allow people to use ICT for meaningful ends.

Some experts consider the digital divide to be merely an economic problem that affects poor countries, although the greatest part of these technologies is manufactured in developing countries, those one who can afford them lack the necessary literacy and knowledge of how to use them. However, identifying the problem exclusively in the economic condition would be inappropriate. The digital divide expresses itself also in the impossibility to use digital technologies within a considerable percentage of the population of industrialized countries . This means that even when people can afford buying a computer or a mobile phone, they do not automatically capable of using it. Another aspect of the digital divide issue is the one that addresses empowerment, which is the ability to fully use the opportunities provided by digital technologies, even if those technologies were accessible and very easy to use , many people would still not be able to take full advantage of their potential.

CONCLUSION

The division of information rich and the information poor is more serious and dangerous than economic stratification of rich and poor. A critique of the notion of a digital divide is necessary to fully inform and make efforts to use technology to promote social inclusion. A framework of technology for social inclusion allows reorienting the focus from that of gaps to be overcome by provision of equipment to that of social development to be enhanced through the effective integration of information and communication technology into communities and institutions. This kind of integration can only be achieved by attention to the wide range of physical, digital, human, and social resources that meaningful access to information and communication technology entails. A society that is free from digital divide and societal divide would have ways for holistic development of a nation and global society.

REFERENCES

1. Compaine, Benjamin M ,Ed. The digital divide: Facing a crisis or creating a myth? Cambridge, MIT Press,2001.
2. Devarajan.G., Information Technology in libraries, New Delhi, Ess Ess Publications, 1999.
3. Vengan.R., *et al,Ed.* Caliber-2000: Information Services in a networked environment in India. Ahmedabad, INFLIBNET Centre, 2000.
4. Wikipedia. http://en.wikipedia.org

Chapter 8

Digital Libraries

INTRODUCTION

The advent of information technology has paved the way for digital libraries. There are a number of terms used by authors to represent the concept of digital library as polyglot library, electronic library, desktop library, on-line library, library without walls, virtual library etc. Of these, digital library is the commonly used terminology by majority of authors. Digital libraries are heterogenous in nature. These include work related to information and how to digitise, store, find, link, visualise, use, publish, manage and share information. Digital libraries provide instant access to digitised information by utilising the avenues of information technology. Today's electronic library based on digitised data is gradually replacing paper - based records and by means of networking one can have access to resources throughout a day. A major advance has been the document delivery service, which transmits by fax the full text of documents unavailable on-line. Unlike printed books, digital libraries are multimedial and data retrievable, can be brought under net-surfing in the sea of information and are aided by hypermedia and hypertext programmes and experimental expert systems.

The use of digital libraries was recognised quite early by the developed countries. But in India it is still at the conceptual level. The aim of this study is to bring out the role of digital libraries in the present day information environment and their new challenges and promises for librarians and library services especially in the Third world countries like India in the 21st century.

GENESIS AND DEVELOPMENT OF DIGITAL LIBRARIES

The origin and development of digital libraries are only three decades of age at the global scenario. Digital libraries are based on minicomputers and they provide basis services for remote access and online search and retrieval. In fact, they make use of techniques to share bibliographic records and link different remote systems. During 1990s there had been a revolution in digital library systems. The technology available today made it possible to mix up media objects such as text, image, audio and video. Because the visual information systems are getting more popular as compared to text-based information systems, digital libraries are becoming more and more graphical in nature. Hypertext technology helps linking references and also helps the information seeker to navigate in the sea of information.

A digital library is a library in which collections are stored in digital formats and accessed by computers. The digital content may be stored locally, or accessed remotely via computer networks. Candela and others define digital library as 'An organization , which might be virtual, that comprehensively collects, manages and preserves for the long term rich digital content, of measurable quality and according to codified policies. The first use of the term digital library in print may have been in a report to the Corporation for National Research Initiatives by Kahn and Cerf. The term digital libraries was first popularized by the

NASA Digital Libraries Initiative in 1994. The term virtual library was initially used interchangeably with digital library, but is now primarily used for libraries that are virtual in other senses.

Digital library is the outcome of information explosion. In 1970s libraries in the developed countries began to connect remote hosts to conduct on-line searches for commercial digital bibliographic databases. The invention of CD-ROM in 1980s was a turning point in the digitisation of information. 1990s marked a progressive move towards digitisation due to networking, electronic document delivery services, on-line services, electronic journals etc.

Digital archives differ from physical libraries in several ways. Traditionally, archives were defined as: i) Containing primary sources of information rather than the secondary sources found in a library ii) Having their contents organized in groups rather than individual items ; iii) Having unique contents.

The technology used to create digital libraries has been more revolutionary for archives since it breaks down the second and third of these general rules. In other words 'digital archives' or 'on-line archives' will still generally contain primary sources , but they are likely to be described individually rather than in groups or collections, and because they are digital their contents are easily reproducible and may indeed have been reproduced from elsewhere. The Oxford Text Archive is generally considered to be the oldest digital archive of academic physical primary source materials

SEMINARS, CONFERENCES AND PROJECTS

Relatively a less number of studies and conferences have been conducted in the various facets of digital libraries. "Library networks and electronic media: challenges for publishers and librarians", Bielfeld University, Germany 8-9

February, 94 was a remarkable conference conducted in the area of digital libraries. In this conference a paper presented by Heinisch brings out the virtual library concept of cyberlib in which all the essential library functions, objects and services are offered in an artificially created, virtual environment. He has also emphasised the overall economics of such a system and ways in which cyberlib could charge users for its services with the clear aim of making a profit and thus entering upon an open and measurable competition with other cyberlibs in order to create a calculable and transparent information market. Another is the international seminar on "Information technologies and information services" organised at Shanghai, Chinese People's Republic, October, 20-24, 1994. In this seminar a paper presented by Lee on Networked, electronic and virtual library discusses the emergence of the networked electronic and virtual library in the USA with particular reference to OCLC. A recent conference is the Libraries without walls organised by the Centre for Research in Library and information Management, Manchester Metropolitan University from 17-20 September 1997 at Lesvos. A number of projects were launched abroad in the area of digital libraries. The MAGIC (Map and Geographic Information Centre of the Homer Babbidge library) attached to the university of Connecticut is a major step in the development of a virtual library. A project entitled "Creating a virtual electronic library" by the University of Illinois Committee on Institutional Cooperation, USA is another project in the field of study. The aim of the project was to create a Virtual Electronic Library (VEL) among 13 major research libraries, develop the technological infrastructure required to provide seamless interconnections among a range of on-line systems and demonstrate its applications through user initiated interlibrary loans by the committee on institutional cooperation (CIC). The virtual library project launched by the Emory University, Atlanta with financial assistance of Luce Foundation for three years explored the ways and means of organisational, economic and educational as well as technological issues to be faced in developing and implementing the prototype of the virtual library.

A notable one- "American memory" project of the Library of Congress aims to make a significant part of its American collections available on on-line by the end of the centuary, at an estimated cost of some $60,000,000.

Large scale digitization projects are underway at Google, the Million Book Project, and Internet Archive. With continued improvements in book handling and presentation technologies such as optical character recognition and e - books, and development of alternative depositories and business models, digital libraries are rapidly growing in popularity as demonstrated by Google, Yahoo, and MSN's efforts Just as libraries have ventured into audio and video collections, so have digital libraries such as the Internet Archive.

According to Larry Lannom, Director of Information Management Technology at the nonprofit Corporation for National Research Initiatives, " all the problems associated with digital libraries are wrapped up in archiving" He goes on to state" If in 100 years people can still read your article, we will have solved the problem". Daniel Akst , author of The Webster Chronicle, proposes that "the future of libraries and information is digital". Peter Lyman and Hal Varian, information scientists at the University of California estimate that "the world's total yearly production of print, film, optical, and magnetic content would require roughly 1.5 billion gigabytes of storage". Therefore , they believe that "soon it will be technologically possible for an average person to access virtually all recorded information".

DIGITAL INFORMATION SEARCHING

Digital libraries provide a search interface which allows resources to be found. These resources are typically invisible web or deep web resources since they frequently cannot be located by search engine crawlers. Some digital libraries create special pages or sitemaps to allow search engines to find all their resources. Koehler states that digital libraries frequently use the Open Archives Initiatives Protocol for Metadata Harvesting(OAI -PMH) to expose their metadata to other digital libraries , and search engines like Google scholar, Yahoo and Scirus can also use OAI-PMH to find these deep web resources.

There are two general strategies for searching a federation of digital libraries such as distributed searching and searching previously harvested metadata.

The distributed searching typically involves a client sending multiple search requests in parallel to a number of servers in the federation. The results are gathered, duplicates are eliminated or clustered, and the remaining items are sorted and presented back to the client. Protocols like Z39.50 are frequently used in distributed searching. A benefit to this approach is that the resource intensive tasks of indexing and storage are left to the respective servers in the federation. A drawback to this approach is that the search mechanism is limited by the different indexing and ranking capabilities of each database, making it difficult to assemble a combined result consisting of the most relevant found items.

Searching over previously harvested metadata involves searching a locally stored index of information that has previously been collected from the libraries in the federation. When a search is performed, the search mechanism doesnot need to make connections with the digital libraries it is searching. This approach requires the creation of an indexing and harvesting mechanism which operates regularly, connecting to all the digital libraries and querying the whole collection in order to discover new and updated resources. OAI-PMH is frequently used by digital libraries for allowing metadata to be harvested. A benefit to this approach is that the search mechanism has full control over indexing and ranking algorithms, possibly allowing more consistent results. A drawback is that harvesting and indexing systems are more resource-intensive and therefore expensive.

SOFTWARE FOR DIGITAL LIBRARY

The digital library can be built around specific repository software. The best known example of this are DSpace, Eprints, Fedora, dLibra, CiteSeerX and Greenstone digital library software. In 2009, Fedora Commons and the DSpace Foundation merged to create a new organization.

ADVANTAGES OF DIGITAL LIBRARIES

The advantages of digital libraries as a means of easily and rapidly accessing books, archives and images of various types are now widely recognized by commercial interests and public bodies alike. Traditional libraries are limited by storage space; digital libraries have the potential to store much more information , simply because digital information requires very little physical space to contain it. As such , the cost of maintaining a digital library is much lower than that of a traditional library. An important advantage to digital conversion is increased accessibility to users. They also increase availability to individuals who may not be traditional patrons of a library, due to geographic location or organizational affiliation. Janet Gertz states the following advantages of digital libraries.

i) No physical boundary. The user of a digital library need not go to the library physically; people from all over the world can gain access to the same information, as long as Internet connection is available.

ii) Round the clock availability. A major advantage of digital libraries is that people can gain access 24/7 to the information.

iii) Multiple access. The same resources can be used simultaneously by a number of institutions and patrons.

iv) Information retrieval. The user is able to use any search term to search the entire collection. Digital libraries can provide very user-friendly interfaces, giving clickable access to its resources.

v) Preservation and conversion. Digitisation is not a long term preservation solution for physical collections , but does succeed in providing access copies for materials that would otherwise fall to degradation from repeated use.

vi) Space. Whereas traditional libraries are limited by storage space, digital libraries have the potential to store much more information , simply because digital information requires very little physical space.

vii) Added value. Certain characteristics of objects, primarily the quality of images , may be improved. Digitaisation can enhance legibility and remove visible flaws such as stains and discolourisation.

ATTEMPTS IN INDIA

Only in the second half of 1990s was the field of study recognised in India. It is worth mentioning here that the 15th Annual convention and conference on Digital libraries was organised by the society for Information Science (New Delhi) at Bangalore from 18-20 January 96. 31 papers on various aspects of digital libraries such as i) Electronic publishers, developers and users, ii) Collecting, capturing, filtering digitised information, iii) Cataloguing, indexing, processing, iv) Networking systems and Electronic access, v) Information professionals for digital information systems, vi) Critical views on effects and achievements, vii) Social, economical and pshychological implications, viii) Indian scenario, problems and prospects etc. were presented at the conference.

The Indian Institute of Science, Bangalore which is considered a pioneer institute in India has established a Digital library. The digital library used the IBM's digital library software running on fast computers. The IISc produces about 1000 papers and around 200 doctoral theses every year. These documents are being made available through digital library. Journals are available in the digitised version. Information sources in CD-ROMs are also available in this digital library.

The efforts of digitisation of Indian petroleum industry and use of electronic communication for geoscientific data and information sources date back to nineteen seventies. Library and information units of Indian petroleum industry, especially the Oil and Natural Gas Commission have evolved various specialised bibliographic databases, on-line public access catalogues of holdings and retrieval services. The efforts are in progress to cover full text of articles and other in house publications, images, maps, graphics animation etc. Other institutions which have taken initiative steps for the establishment of digital library are National Informatics Centre, All India Institute of Medical Sciences in New Delhi, National Institute of Mental Health and Neurosciences in Bangalore and MGR University.

CHALLENGES AND PROMISES

The above observations will make clear that books and libraries are in transition and the library profession in India should undergo inevitable changes in the 21st centuary. It is beyond doubt that the digital library concept offers almost unlimited opportunities to devise new and innovative services and the profession stands to gain immensely from the development of the virtual library.

Librarians should visualise their future and that of their libraries and information services in terms of merging of libraries with computer technology and telecommunications into a virtual library. In this respect the future librarians should have to become more active, harnessing the resources of the electronic world rather than simply learning about them. Also librarians must ask themselves how the routine ways of doing things might be done differently in the new context of work and in the present information environment. The arrival of INTERNET would compel librarians to learn a new range of skills in navigating in the sea of information.

PROBLEMS

The digitisation of information sources and ultimate result of developing digital library raise strong arguments in favour of a change from conventional documents to digital forms. Despite all the aforesaid advantages of digitisation, whether the libraries in the Third world countries like India are mature enough for such an immediate transition? In respect of modernisation of libraries the developing countries are years back when compared with libraries in the developed countries. Developing countries like India face a number of problems in materialising the concept of digital libraries. They are the following:

i) The developed countries are the major producers of digitised information sources which lack coverage of literature produced from Third world countries;

ii) Fiscal allocation in libraries is not always in tune with the inflation;

iii) Imbalance between the manpower produced in library science schools and the manpower requirements in libraries;

iv) Lack of indigenous, efficient and effective library software packages;

v) Lack of information policy and information culture;

vi) Lack of information audit in libraries and information centres; and

vii) Problems relating to the conversion of the existing manual data bases into computer-readable databases.

The digitisation of information is inevitable and a "necessary evil" in the present day information world. The avenues of information technology help libraries in reducing the size of the library from big to small. The smallness of the library due to the digitisation of information will overcome a number of problems faced by the traditional libraries. But a total transformation of libraries into digital libraries all on a sudden is not possible, feasible and not a wise decision in the case of libraries in Third world countries like India due to a number of interrelated socio-economic and political factors. But we should not shut our eyes towards the fast developing technological changes in the information arena. Of course, the digital libraries revolutionised the traditional libraries by digitising and displaying into the computer monitor in the houses of users the information sources of the libraries. As a result of this in future it may not be necessary for a user to visit the library for information!

REFERENCES

1. Akst, D : The digital library : Its future has arrived. Carnegie Reporter.2(3) PP.4-8

2. Candela, L, et al: The DELOS digital library reference model - foundations for digital libraries. version 0.98 February 2008.

3. Centre for Research in Library and Information Management (Manchester): Conference Proceedings on Libraries without walls, 17-20 September, 1997.

4. Edward A Fox: The digital libraries initiative -update and discussion, Bulletin of the American Society of Information Science.26(1)1999.

5. Emory University, Atlanta: Virtual library project. Atlanta, Emory University, 1994.

6. Gertz, Janet: Selection for preservation in the digital age. Library Resources & Technical services.44(2) 2000.PP. 97-104

7. Heinish.C : Cyberlib: Vision and economic analysis. Libri.44(4)1994.p.393-99.

8. Kahn, RE and CERF, VG : The digital library project vol.1 - The world of knowbots,1988.

9. Koehler, AEC: Some thoughts on the meaning of open access for university library technical services serials review. 32(1)2006

10. Lee.H.W.: Networked, electronic and virtual library: Libraries of the 1990s.Jl.of Educational Media and Library sciences. 32(2)95.p.119-29.

11. Malwad,N.M.,et al, ed: Digital libraries: Dynamic store house of digitised information. New Delhi, New Age International, 1996.p.270.

12. Malwad.N.M.,et al ed: Digital libraries: Dynamic storehouse of digitized information. New Delhi, New Age International, 1996.

13. McGlammery.P.: Magic at the University of Connecticut:

Building the virtual map library Geography and map division Bulletin.179.1995.p.14-30.

14. Polley.J.A. and Lyon.E: out of the archives and into the street: American memory in American libraries. Online. 16(5)1992.p.51-57.

15. University of Illinois Committee on Institutional Cooperation, USA: Creating a virtual electronic library.

Chapter 9

Library Software Packages

INTRODUCTION

A software is a set of programmes written or developed to enable the computer to do desired operations. The software can be broadly categorised into two types: system software and application software. The system softwares are otherwise known as operating systems which are sets of programmes inbuilt in computers to run the computer whereas application softwares are used in the computer to perform specific applications. In the case of libraries application softwares are used to automate house keeping operations such as aquisition, technical processing, circulation, serials control etc. Today, quite a number of library software packages are available for librarians for house keeping operations and information storage and retrieval purposes. For developing in-house software to solve complex problems, the requirements become severe and unmanageable. Because of these limitations, practicing libraries or information scientists should be exposed to some commercially available software packages.

The softwares are also categorised, based on their functions, such as i) Basic software for data entry, validation etc; ii) word processing software to manipulate text-storage; iii) Data base management systems (DBMS) for management of databases; iv) Text-Retrieval packages for storage and retrieval on non-numeric records; v) software associated with searching on-line retrieval system and CD-ROM databases; and vi) Library House keeping software.

This chapter is intended to give an account of major library software packages and their important features. This chapter also provides certain guide lines as the criteria for the selection of library software packages.

LIBRARY SOFTWARE PACKAGES DEVELOPED IN FOREIGN COUNTRIES

The developed countries are in the forefront in the development of library software packages. There are a number of library software packages developed during 1980s and 1990s which are being used in libraries internationally in library automation. An account of such major library software packages are given below.

OASIS/ALICE PACKAGES

These are two important packages developed by international Group- Softlink America and Softlink- Australia. This software is introduced in India by the Softlink Asia Pvt. Ltd. The OASIS package run under DOS platform and Alice run under Windows platform. These packages are used in more than 7000 major libraries all over the world. OASIS/Alice software packages perform various library functions like Management, Acquisition, Circulation, On-line Public Access Catalogue (OPAC), periodical and Journal Indexing, Stock verification etc.

The main features of the OASIS/Alice packages are the following:

i) OASIS/Alice is a menu driven package which facilitates easy use by both library staff and users;

ii) It has simple search screen. So the users can carry out simple as well as complex search, print the result and on-line reservation;

iii) The search screen has password. This will protect the system so that the end-user cannot enter into database design area;

iv) It takes care of all library functions. This will fecilitate fileless library;

v) It runs on Bar Code Technology which facilitates speedy circulation of books and stock verification;

vi) It runs on multiuser platform. It supports Novell Netware, Windows NT system on DOS, Windows 3.1 or 95 or Windows 98;

vii) It also runs on single user platform convertible to multiuser platform;

viii) It has inbuilt communication. It facilitates on-line access to other libraries;

ix) It has CD-ROM loader. It facilitates downloading data from CD-ROM diskettes;

x) It has multimedia function. It facilitates scanning of data, videos, graphics, photographs, sound clips in records etc;

xi) It has 7 digit data capacity. This enables it to hold 99 lakh records;

xii) It has special data protection. It facilitates saving of data upto last record entered in case of power failure;

xiii) It has inbuilt tutorial modules. It helps library staff/ students to learn the software by themselves;

xiv) It has complete documentation. The reference manuals and tutorial manuals help the library staff to understand the software functions and the library automation.

Alice for Windows provides a complete range of functions packed in discrete modules. It is configurable to suit the working practices of individual libraries and may be operated as a single user system or as a true multiuser system. It also works efficiently under Windows NT environment. Softlink international provides Web enquiry module to facilitate global information search from any corner of the globe and from any platform DOS/UNIX/ Windows in library Data Base.

CDS/ISIS

The acronym CDS/ISIS stands for Computerised Documentation System/Integrated Set of Information System. It is a menu-driven generalised information storage and retrieval system, designed specifically for computerised management of databases. It has designed and developed by UNESCO's Division of Software Development Applications Office of Information Programmes and Services. NISSAT is the national distributor of this package in India.

NISSAT is also financing various organisations for imparting training programmes to library personnel in using this package. The software is highly useful and fast in creating bibliographical databases for information storage and retrieval. But, the menus provides in the software are not adequate for library housekeeping operations. Nevertheless, the software allows creation of additional menus for such operations through writing programmes in pascal language. The important features of this package are:

i) the package allows its users to create non-numerical databases;

ii) the database can contain over one crore sixty lakh records;

iii) the maximum size of display format is of 4,000 characters;

iv) there are menus and sub menus which provide options;

v) it allows the user to create data base/s on his/her own;

vi) it allows the user to enter new records in a database and edit, modify, delete, print, display or browse the existing records;

vii) the status information is displayed as soon as a database is selected;

viii) its indexing capabilities are extremely dependable and fast;

ix) its search facilities are simple, accurate and rapid;

x) details of search results can be seen immediately on VDU and also can be printed/copied.

xi) it allows the users to make their own menus or sub-menus and their own programmes through advance programming.

Some of the disadvanges of the package are listed below:

i) A user has to use separate menus to modify or remove data while searching which is a lenghthy process.

ii) The software is not suitable for graphic information

iii) There is no facility for viewing different records simultaneously.

iv) One Field Definition Table (FDT) can be used only for one database.

v) Regeneration of serial numbers after sorting the

entries is not possible.

vi) There is no facility to control the right margin in printing.

PROCITE 3.1 FOR WINDOWS

The ProCite 3.1 for Window is a Reference database management system developed by Personal Bibliographic Software, Inc, Ann Arbor. As a reference data base management system, it provides a number of features. Through its available and developing integration with work processors, it offers much needed functionally supporting the generation in-text citation, footnotes and bibliographies.

There are about 50,000 registered users of ProCite worldwide. It is used by scholars and professional librarians. Among them there are such corporate users as Dow Chemical Corporation. Allied Signal and Astramerck pharmaceuticals. This software maintains a World Wide Web site with information on its products. As a Window product, ProCite 3.1 makes execellent use of graphical user interface. The database screen can be customised to make information easy to find.

Biblio-Link II is a companion product for ProCite 3.1. When installed, it enhanced ProCite 3.1's importing capabilities. Biblio-link provides instructions for down loading and filters for importing from several on-line bibliographic sources and CD-ROM sources. Filters and instructions are provided for importing from DIALOG, MEDLARS and STN International etc. Insturctions are also provided for modifying existing filters or creating new filters to allow for better record importing, if needed.

MINISIS

This software is developed by International

Development Centre (IDRC) Canada. It works on HP 300 family of computers. It is a useful package for library work including networking. It is an efficient application software package for big libraries. In India this software can be had from Hewlett Packard India Ltd., Community Centre, New Delhi.

CITATION 7

The Citation 7 is a datafile manager and bibliographic citation generator. This has been developed by Noteoberon, New York. The main feature of this software is that it works from within Word Perfect for Windows and Microsoft Word and is accessed from the tools menu of these word processors. Another important feature of Citation 7 is its capability of formatting the selected items in a data file into a desired bibliographical format.

END NOTE PLUS

This is an enhanced referenced database and bibliography manager. This software was developed by Niles and Associates, Inc, Berkeley. According to the vendor there are over 85,000 registered users for End Note Plus 2. It requires Windows 95 or Windows NT as operating system.

The End Note Plus 2 makes good use of the graphical user interface. The user has the option of using menu bars or key-combinations to perform various tasks within the programme.

CONSEARCH 3.0

This is an Electronic Research and Utility for Windows. It was developed by Management Information Technologies, Inc, Hauppauge, New York. There are about 1000 registered users for Consearch. Consearch runs on Windows platform and it has good use of the graphical user interface.

TOTAL LIBRARY COMPUTERISATION (TLC) VERSION 2

This software package was developed by On Point, Inc, Washington DC for automation of small and medium sized libraries. TLC runs on single user and multi-user environment. TLC has basic library management modules for catalouging, circulation, serials control, acquisition etc.

THE LIBRARY PROGRAM

The library program is a DOS-based group of programs produced and distributed by Microcomputer Business Systems of Amity, Oregon. There are over 200 users of the Library Program. Of these 70% are church libraries and 30% school libraries. The major features of the software include: provision for basic security through user account model; adding a user's name to the program and setting his or her password in an easy process; and once a user is logged in; the program access is set and is not reset until the next user logs in. A limitation of the LIBRARY PROGRAM is that it does not offer on-line public access catalogue (OPAC).

In addition to the softwares mentioned above, packages such as "Circulation, Catalog Plus and Alliance Plus" suitable for school libraries, "Athena" a Window-based integrated library system developed by Nichols Advanced Technologies for school libraries etc are other important library software packages from western fields.

INDIAN LIBRARY SOFTWARE PACKAGES

There are a number of indigenous library packages developed by library professionals or computer experts for inhouse use of library automation for specific functions. Some agencies have developed library softwares on a commercial basis for general application in libraries. A brief account of commercially available library software packages in India are given under.

SANJAY

Sanjay is an augumented version of CDS/ISIS. CDS/ISIS is a generalised information storage and retrieval software for the management of structured non-numerical databases. It cannot be used strightaway for the management of house-keeping operations. But the CDS/ISIS has provision for interfacing the necessary software modules with it for covering the house-keeping operations. Hence NISSAT, the distributing agency in India for CDS/ISIS package, has become interested in getting the modules for library house-keeping operations developed indigenously. So NISSAT has awarded a project to DESIDOC for the development of these additional modules in PASCAL. Accordingly DESIDOC has developed the additional modules for the library house-keeping applications on CDS/ISIS. This package is called SANJAY. It is an integrated package that enhances the capabilities of CDS/ISIS by interfacing pascal programmes. The SANJAY performs the library management functions such as Acquisition control, on-line catalogue management, Circulation control etc. The main features of SANJAY are : i) the package is capable of handling numerical operations like calculation of budgetry allocations and expenditure; ii) it provides linking of two or more databases for a single application, like linking an acquisition system with the on-line catalogue and circulation system; iii) the inverted files are updated automatically whenever a change is made in the database; iv) it has a set of 70 pascal programmes and 25 special menus; v) faster response time; vi) new menus can be inserted in between the existing menus without affecting their functions.

LIBSYS

This package was developed by Lybsys corporation, New Delhi. It is a fully integrated multi-user library system designed to run on a wide spectrum of hardware/software platforms in client-server environment. It is easy to operate and the library staff can begin to use it quickly without much computer skills. It ensures high productivity because of minimal data entry requirements, maximum possible integration of functions and powerful search and query facilities. It has its own centralised bibliographic database based on ANSI Z39.50 format. LIBSYS supports almost all activities relating to acquisition, cataloguing, circulation and serials control and has a powerful but at the same time user friendly OPAC interface.

LIbsys is highly user-friendly having features such as integrated functions, interactive and screen oriented, menu driven, multi-user capabilities, minimum possible data entry, powerful data editing facility, easily installable, user defined security, database recovery proceedure, help facility etc. LIbsys is well proved software having more than 120 registered users in South Asian countries, since 1988. The registered users include universities, public libraries, Governmental organisations, British libraries etc.

MAITREYI

This software was developed by Computer Maintenance Corporation (CMC) for Calcutta Library Network (CALIBNET). This provides facilities for all jobs relating to housekeeping and information storage and retrieval fuctions. This software can be purchased from CMC, Calcutta.

Wylisys

Wylisys stands for WIpro Library System. It was developed by Wipro Computer Ltd. It has facilities for housekeeping and information storage and retrieval functions.

DELMS

Defence Library Management System (DELMS) was developed by DESIDOC as an in-house software package for library use. It has facilities for working on UNIX, XENIX and DOS flatforms.

ILMS

This software was developed by INFLIBNET centre Ahammadabad. This software was developed as a means to automate the documentary resources available in all the university libraries and college libraries in India under the INFLIBNET programme. Because of some problems the package could not be used by librarians on a satisfactory level. So this package is not in vogue.

ARCHIVES

ARCHIVES is an integrated software package developed in multi-user FOXPRO based by Minifax Electronics Pvt. Ltd., Bombay. It is a comprehensive package offering acquisition control, serial control, cataloguing, circulation control, information storage and retrieval and SDI.

LIBMAN

LIBMAN was developed by Datapro Consltancy services, Pune. Creation of database of books, members, issue and return, interlibrary loan, generation of overdue lists, computerisation of figures etc are possible with this package.

LIBRA

It is a multiuser, multilingual, userfriendly package

available from Ivy Systems Ltd, New Delhi. It facilitates house keeping operations such as acquisition control, circulation control, cataloging and on-line retrieval.

LIBRARIAN

Librarian is library management software package developed by computer professionals in consultation with experienced library professionals. It was developed by Soft-Aid, Pune.

LIBRIS

Lybris is a comprehensive, user friendly and menu driven library software package developed by Frontier Information Technologies Pvt.Ltd., Secunderabad. The system covers all the functional activities such as acquisition, cataloguing, circulation, serials control, enquires and library administration.

MEMLIB

The Memex Library Manager (Memlib) was developed by Memox, Pvt. Ltd., New Delhi. It is a microsoft windows based, application software which can run in a single user or multi-user environment. This software provides facilities for almost all important functions in a library. This includes acquisition, processing, circulation, serials control etc. Another important feature of this software is its import facility of CDS/ISIS database. Memlib on-line search facility provides for various options and makes many selected jobs easy without browsing entirely through the data and makes the job very easy.

KRVGER LIBRARY MANAGER

It is a menu-driven and user-friendly software

developed by Blitz Auto Visuals, Pune. It is a complete library management package for on-line information. It runs on PC XT/AT compatibles. It contains facilities for validation of data entry, circulation control, catalogue card printing, information services, preparation of cards according to AACR II, information search etc.

TRISHNA

It was developed by NISTADS, New Delhi, Trishna- is a version of CDS/ISIS. It supports data creation, storage and retrieval in Indian languages.

ULYSIS

Universal Library System (Ulysis) was developed by Wipro Information Technology Ltd. The package is developed in C language. It is a fully integrated system taking care of house-keeping and information storage and retrieval functions.

SOUL

The SOUL (Software for University Libraries) is a library software package developed by INFLIBNET Centre, an IUC of University Grants Commission, Ahmedabad as a total solution for library automation and management. The SOUL is designed using client-server Architecture, which imparts extra strength to storage capacity, and has multiple access to single database, various levels of security, back up and restorage facilities etc. This software was designed after a comprehensive study of different library related functions practised in university libraries. It has MS-SQL Server 6.5 RDMS as the back end. This user friendly software is quite easy to work. The software contains modules viz Acquisition, Catalogue, Circulation, OPAC, Serials Control and Administration.

The in-built network features of the software will allow multiple libraries of the universities to function together and access to distributed databases installed at various university libraries and union catalogue mounted at INFLIBNET using VAST network.

The acquisition module enables library staff to handle the following major functions of library materials viz i) suggestion management; ii) ordering, cancellation and reminders; iii) receiving; iv) payment including fund control; and v) master file management such as currency table, vendors, publisher, user etc.

The catalogue module is used for retrospective conversion of books; technical processing of books received from Acquisition section, printing a range of records for verification, searching by title and accession numbers, the authority files for publishers etc. One of the unique features of SOUL is its access to authority files on screen as well as selection box in various fields of records. Once the proposed VAST Network by INFLIBNET is commissioned, this module will take care of automatic replication of data into union catalogue. This will avoid exchange of library data on physical media i.e floppy, tape etc. This module covers the functions such as catalogue process, catalogue search, user services, catalogue card generation, authority file maintenance, retro conversion, stock verification report generation, union data base maintenance; and export/ import of records.

The circulation module will take care of all possible functions dealt in a university library set up. Starting from membership management, maintenance of status of library items can be handled using SOUL. The circulation transactions viz issue, return, renewal, reserve, recall, hold can be done successfully. The complex functions like fine management for each category of user and material can also be effectively carried out. Inter library loan, searching the status of every member or library item is also possible. Remainders for overdue material, generation of various reports have also been covered.

The On-line Public Access catalogue (OPAC) of SOUL is a window to the library collection. Using the user friendly menu, user can search for an item available in the library by author, title, corporate author, conference name, subject descriptor, Class number etc. The Boolean search enables the user to conduct the search using all combinations including type of material, language, year etc. Besides, this will serve as first point of information about the library and laos gateway for accessing INTERNET, union data base or any other external sources.

The complex job of keeping serials control is effectively handled by serials control module. This module handles the functions such as suggestions, subscription, payment including fund control, check of uses, issue arrival, reminder generation, binding management, search status of every item, master data base management, report generation etc.

User administration module is used for creating new users and giving them right for accessing different modules.

The SOUL is available in stand alone and network versions. It is a suitable package to work under university environment. Moreover, the network feature of the software will allow multiple libraries of university to function together.

PALMS (PRASAD AUTOMATED LIBRARY MANAGEMENT SYSTEMS)

This package was developed by Dr.R C Prasad, Scientist (Library and Documentation, GBPIHED) and it is distributed by Nutan Software & Publishing, Almora U.P. It is a menu-driven user-friendly single and multiuser networking package runs under DOS environment. It is hoped that the package is very useful to automate all types of libraries, small or big. The package will also be useful to scientists/researchers in maintaining the references related to the field of research. This package is used for database management and for information services such as SDI, current awareness services and Bibliographical services.

Other features of the package include report generation, utilities and tools, automatic book number system, data protection, fast speed, query facilities, compatability with other software packages etc.

ODYSSEY

This software was developed by SRA System Ltd, Imaging Division, Chennai. It is a comprehensive Document Image Management System which provides easy methods for storage, sharing and retrieval of documents. It takes information from various sources such as scanners, faxes, computer created documents and other ASC II files. It supports various types of storage media like Hard Discs, Optical Disks, CD-ROMs and Juke Boxes. It uses an advanced Database Engine to store, retrieve indices and provides multiple searching mechanism like QBE, Wild Cards, Boolean Operators and Keywords.

The main features of the software are the following:

i) It provides multi-level security features and access control for the document images.

ii) It supports different types of scanners and provides a flexible scanner control

iii) It uses CCITT Group IV Fax format for compression of B/W documents and JPEC format for colour documents.

iv) It allows the users to index their document in a flexible manner with user definable index fields which could be used later for retrieval. Text index can also be built automatically using the OCR facility.

v) It provides document archival facilities including archival management- Read/Write disk cache, batch mode archival, read only and re-writable disk management, auto servicing of requests for retrieval and volume management etc.

vi) It provides a comprehensive electronic filing cabinet in a hieararchical fashion. Document can also be filed automatically in multiple folders without duplication.

vii) It provides various methods of retrieval by unique system generated ID number, document reference, key words, text search facility, Query by form (QBF) for document types etc.

viii) It provides notepad facility to annotate on document images.

ix) It has a built in mailing system. This enables users to mail documents with messages within the ODYSSEY network. It also supports CC Mail and MS Mail.

x) It incorporates a work-Flow facility, using which any user can initiate an action oriented document routing process to route documents to other users in the network. The user will also be able to keep track of documents and their flow when they move from one user to another.

xi) OCR can be used for text search, conversion of image text to ASCII text, content based text search and automatic indexing.

xii) It contains a comprehensive Text search facility to provide support for content based search using OCR facility. Text search can also be performed on ASCII text and word processed documents for content based retrieval.

xiii) It provides utilities for data export and import through ASCII format.

xiv) ODYSSEY is built around client-server architecture and supports NetBIOS, SPX/IPX and TCP/IP communication protocols.

xv) It is developed with modular and open-ended design; therefore it can easily be integrated with other application software systems.

The system requirements for ODYSSEY application are: PC/AT 486 or above, 8MB RAM, VGA Display, MS Windows 3.0/ Windows 95/Windows NT, and industry standard scanner.

In addition to the indigenous software listed above a number of library software packages have been designed by library professionals with the assistance of computer experts for in-house library use. But attempt is not made herein to give details due to lack of documentation about these packages.

FREE SOFTWARE

Free software or open software is software that can be used, studied, and modified without restriction, and which can be copied and redistributed in modified or unmodified from either without restriction , or with minimal restrictions only to ensure that further recipients can also do these things and that manufacturers of consumer facing hardware. Free software is generally available without charge, but can have a fee. In practice, for software to be distributed as free software , the human-readable form of the programme (the source code) must be made available to the recipient along with a notice granting the above permissions. Such a notice is either a 'free softwarelicense' or a notice that the source code is released into the public domain. The definition written by Richard Stallman, is still maintained and states that software is free software if people who receive a copy of the software have the following four freedoms

- Freedom 0: The freedom to run the programme for any purpose
- Freedom 1: The freedom to study how the programme works, and change it to make it do what you wish.
- Freedom 2: The freedom to redistribute copies so you can help your neighbour.
- Freedom 3: The freedom to improve the programme , and release your improvements to the public, so that the whole community benefits.

The free software Directory maintains a large database of free software packages. Some of the best known examples include the Linux Kernel, the BSD and GNU/Linux operating systems, the GNU Compiler Collection and C Library ; the MYSQL relational database; the Apache web server; and the sendmail mail transport agent. Other examples include the emacs text editor; the GIMP raster drawing and image editor; the X Windows System graphical-display system; the Open Office.org office suite; and the TeX and LaTeX typesetting systems.

CRITERIA FOR SELECTION OF LIBRARY SOFTWARE PACKAGE

The discussion made above will reveal that quite a number of library software packages both foreign and indigenous are available to librarians for automation. But the question is whether a librarian should go for a library package in-house developed by the computer experts available in his institution or go for purchase of a commercially available package? The software developed through in-house and that available from market have their on merits and demerits. In the case of software developed by in-house experts, they are not usually developed scientifically and tested by time in its use. But of course, the cost is less in the development of such packages. Whereas in the case of software developed by commercial agencies they are developed as a result of team research and tested by time and most of these packages have general application and are suitable for all types of libraries. But the cost is high in the case of commercially available library software packages. So in the light of expert opinion and experiences it is better to go for purchase of a commercially available package for library automation. Then the next question before librarian is which library software package should be purchased out of the large number of packages that are available through commercial channel? What are the criteria or checklist to be considered in the selection of software packages? Computerisation of a library requires a lot of money, manpower and materials. The computerised library system may affect positively or negatively the efficiency of a library because of the particular software package used by library. Hence an objective assesment or evaluation of the packages is required in the choice of particular software for automation.

The general guidelines for the selection of a commercially available software package are the following:

i) Located and evaluate a knowledgeable dealer or sales person.

ii) Thoroughly examine the documentation for the software you are considering.

iii) Arrange for a demonstration of the software.

iv) Prepare yourself before the demonstration.

v) Put the programme through its paces.

vi) Evaluate the quality of the support you can expect from the dealer or vendor.

According to Glossbrener the following are the rules or guidelines for the selection of a software.

i) Do not take anything for granted.

ii) You are not the stupid one

iii) How many and how long? How many author names can you put in the file? How long can each name be?

iv) Forget about the sizzle and focus on the steak. Ask, what the programme can do and how well it can do it?

v) Whenever possible, make an effort to visualise yourself using the programme.

vi) Read at least two reviews of any programme before you buy.

vii) Get a demonstration on the indentical computer, configured exactly as the one you will be using.

viii) Life will be easier if you stick with proven products offered by major hardware and software firms.

ix) Buy only the four "building block" programmes to start with. The four building block programmes are communications, word processing, electronic spreadsheet and personal database management.

x) Don't drive yourself crazy trying to get something to work.

xi) Nothing is impossible. But the game may not be worth the candle. Computers and software are so versatile that you can accomplish just about anything you want

xii) Whenever you can-wait! Make sure the rapidly changing software market works for you.

The publication entitled Library systems Evaluation Guide listed the following guidelines as the phases for the selection of a library software package for library automation especially for house keeping operations.

Phase 1: Setting objectives.

Phase 2: Fine tuning of components of the methodology to agree with objectives.

Phase 3: Selection of candidate systems for evaluation.

Phase 4: Examination of accompanying system literature and documentation.

Phase 5: Comparison of candidate systems with the functions and features, table and with the checklist of data elements.

Phase 6: On-site evaluation of candidate systems.

Phase 7: System selection and acquisition.

Phase 8: Post-installation evaluation.

Rowley provides a checklist for the selection of a checklist for the selection of a software package under the following three heads viz General Criteria, Technical criteria and support criteria.

The general criteria include i) Others' experience, ii) cost, iii) Originator, iv) and supplier. The technical criteria include language, operating system, hardware, ease-in-use and format. The support criteria include documentation, advice to setting up the package, training in the use of software package, maintenance and user group meets etc.

According to Grosch the following are some of the important criteria for the selection of software packages. Grosch has pointed out the availability of the capabilities and product enhancements of the application software at the time of installation. Other criteria include: examining hardware platform options, operating system requirements, direction of the system developers towards open systems, conversion support, record of the old and new versions of the software, ease of use etc.

CONCLUSION

In general, the selection or choice of anything is a difficult job. In the case of software selection each software has its own merits and demerits. It is the duty of the liabrarian to assess the positive and negative aspects of the software package and select an appropriate one which is suitable for the library. In fact the selection of the software, aspects such as the objective of the library, collection, services to be generated from the library, user-friendly nature of the software, cost, compatibility, authoritativeness of the firm which produced the software, after sales service support etc should be considered.

REFERENCES

1. DESIDOC: SANJAY User Guide.New Delhi, DESIDOC, 1991.
2. Grosch, Andrey: In evaluation procurement and other factors affecting the Shaping of your library system. New York, Marcel Dekker,1995
3. James, J: Library systems evaluation guide .v8.Ohio, Rush Associates, 1983
4. LYBSYS: Pamphlet. New Delhi, Lybsys Corporation
5. Malwad.N.M: Selection criteria for library automation software. Desidoc Bulletin.15 (2) 1995.p.17-25.
6. Rowley, J: Automation options. In handbook of special librarianship and information Work. Ed.6.London, Meckler, 1989.
7. Seghal.R.L: Handbook of library software packages. New Delhi, ESS ESS, 1998..

Chapter 10

Information Technology in LIS Curriculum Design

INTRODUCTION

The revision of library and information science curriculum is a major issue of great concern today. Library science schools have been adapting the curricula incorporating the recent developments taking place in the domain of the fast developing subject. The library schools in the developed countries have been revising the curriculum so frequently as to meet the new challenges in the information world. But such a revision of the curriculum of the library schools in the Third world countries has not been frequently done in order to meet the rapid changes taking place in the information world. In fact the developments in the field are so fast that the library schools could not even keep pace with the revision of curriculum. This situation creates quite a lot of mismatching between the manpower generated from library schools and the actual manpower requirements in libraries and information centres in the third world countries like India. Considering this aspect, an attempt is made in this chapter to examine how far the existing curriculum in library schools respond to the new changes taking place especially in the field of information technology and in generating need-based manpower requirements in libraries and information centres in India.

LIBRARY AND INFORMATION SCIENCE EDUCATION IN INDIA

As a prelude to the topic of discussion a brief account of library science education in India is provided here.

Next to USA, India is the country which established the largest number of library science schools. India recognised the importance of library science education relatively quite early because of the demand for qualified manpower requirement felt in the management of various types of libraries. Mr.W.A.Borden, an American librarian brought by Maharaja Sayajerao Gackwad of Baroda to organise a library system in his princely State started a training programme in 1911. At present about 78 universities offer various level of courses in Library and Information Science in India.

LEVELS OF LIBRARY SCIENCE COURSES IN INDIA

Universities, governmental agencies, autonomous colleges, professional organisations etc conduct various levels of courses in Library and Information Science. The majority of the courses are offered through formal channel. It is also offered through non-formal education channel such as correspondance and distance education. The following are the various levels of courses offered in India.

(i) Certificate/Diploma in Library Science (c.lib.sc/ Dip.Lib.sc)

Universities, governmental agencies, autonomous colleges, professional organisations etc conduct various levels of courses in Library and Information Science. A few universities and other governmental agencies also conduct certificate courses. The duration of the course is 4 months. A few autonomous colleges conduct one year diploma in library science. The course content is focused mainly on aspects of traditional librarianship such as library organisation and administration, library classification theory and practice, library cataloging theory and practice etc. These courses will be helpful only in supplying semi-professional positions in various types of libraries.

ii) Graduate Level Courses (B.L.I.Sc)

Universities are main agencies in the conduct of graduate level one year course viz Bachelor of Library and Information Science (B.L.I.Sc). Now a few colleges affiliated to the various universities in the country also conduct B.L.I.Sc. The universities viz Madras, Annamalai, Madurai, Calicut and Open Universities viz A.P. Open University and Indira Gandhi National Open University offer B.L.I.Sc through correspondance and distance education channels. Now about 78 universities in India offer B.L.I.Sc course for the supply of professional manpower required in various types of libraries. The course contents include Library and Society, Library Management, Reference sources and services, Library Classification theory and practice, and Library Cataloging theory and practice. The syllabi of B.L.I.Sc. course in some of the universities include a separate paper on Library Automation/Information Technology. But some of the universities have included these aspects in the syllabi only as part of Information service paper.

iii) Post-graduate Level Courses(M.L.I.Sc/M.L.I.S)

About 43 universities in India offer post-graduate level courses viz M.L.I.Sc/M.L.I.S in Library and Information Science. Universities such as Madras, Annamalai, Madurai, Kerala and Indira Gandhi National Open universities conduct P.G. programmes through correspondence and distance education. The duration of the course is one year in majority of the library schools. But universities viz Madras, Mysore, Mangalore, North-East Hill universities, Kerala, Calicut etc offer M.L.I.Sc programme as a two-year integrated course. The course contents include aspects on traditional librarianship, Information science and information technology. Now most of the library science schools include information technology as separate paper/s in the syllabi. The objective of this course is to generate manpower required in the senior positions in the library field.

iv) Research Level Programmes

M.phil and Ph.D are the research level programmes conducted in India. The universities viz Delhi, Gulbarga, S.V, Annamalai, Madurai and Kerala universities offer one year M.phil programme in Library and Information Science. There are three papers and one dissertation in the M.phil curricula. Research methodology is a common paper and bibliometrics, comparative librarianship or library science education , or Library Management are the other papers included in the programme. More than 30 universities offer Ph.D programmes. A few universities in India also offer post-doctoral programmes in library and information science leading to D.Litt

v) Specialized Courses

A few library schools/university level institutions in India conduct specialized courses in the area of documentation, information science, library automation, information technology etc which differ from the general stream. They are:

(i) M.Sc: It is a 2 year course in Information Science conducted by the Birla Institute of Technology, Ranchi, Bihar and M.Sc in Information Technology by the Guru Jhambeswar University, Hissar, Haryana.

(ii) Associateship in Documentation and Information Science (ADIS) by the DRTC, Bangalore and Associateship in Information Science (AIS) by NISCAIR,

New Delhi.

(iii) One year training in computer applications in library and information services by the National Centre for Science Information, Indian Institute of Science, Banglore.

(iv) One year diploma in library automation/information technology. The one year post M.L.I.Sc Diploma in Library Automation by the University of Mysore and one year Post-Graduate Diploma in Information Technology (PGDIT) by the University of Kerala also come under this category. Diploma in information technology by the Central University, Hyderabad is a specialized course conducted through distance education.

EVALUATION OF THE PRESENT CURRICULUM IN LIBRARY SCHOOLS IN INDIA

Curriculum is the planned interaction of students with instructional content, instructional resources and instructional processes for the attainment of pre determined educational objectives. It must be liberal enough to accommodate a radical reconstruction of the objectives of education and also to cover the introduction of new methods of teaching and learning. The curriculum in Library and Information Science schools in India needs timely revision and development. The development of curriculum in library and information science education is needed primarly because library and information science as a discipline is still in the process of emerging in India. Several areas of library and information science are yet to be developed. As new knowledge in library and information science grows, new discoveries are made, and known facts are scientifically organised and interpreted, the development of curriculum for library and information science becomes imperative. Another reason for curriculum development in library and information science is the changing information environment. The curriculum planners have to ascertain what new objectives are to be selected for meeting the emerging needs; what new knowledge could be used to realise the objectives; and what new learning experience could be offered to learners to make education more meaningful and to meet the new challenges of modern times. In fact the design and structure of the curriculum should be planned scientifically to assure continuity, balance, harmony and unity in the educational programme.

The regional seminar organised by the (ASTINFO) on Information Education strategies for the 21st century held in Beijing in September 1995 pointed out a number of problems in library science schools in South Asian region. They are:

i) Shortage of information professionals skilled in using information technology;

ii) Lack of inservice training facilities for librarians in computing and telecommunications;

iii) Insufficient attention to the needs of the various sectors of the economy, especially those of industry;

iv) Lack of attractiveness of information science programme for the best students;

v) Infrequent revision of existing curricula;

vi) Shortage of qualified staff;

vii) Paucity of financial resources for both teaching institutions and students.

An ideal curriculum should contain the following three dimentional attributes.

i) A systematic group of courses or sequences of subjects required for graduation or certification in a major field of study;

ii) A general overall plan of the content or specific materials of instruction that the school should offer to the student by way of qualifying him for graduation or certification or for entrance into a professional or vocational field;

iii) A body of prescribed educative experiences under school supervision, designed to provide an individual with the best possible training and experience to fit him for the society of which he is a part or to qualify him for a trade or profession. In fact, the curriculum takes into account the factors such as i) needs of the students ii) the content iii) instructional methodology; and criteria for evaluation of students' performance.

THE STRUCTURE OF CURRICULUM FOR 21ST CENTUARY

An objective evaluation of the above said aspects has become so imperative in question relating to curriculum design in library science schools in India. The existing curriculum can create only "half-baked professionals" or "broiler librarians" for the 21st centuary unless we are willing to change our attitude towards the revision of curriculum in Library and Information Science schools in the Developing countries. What should be the structure and features of the curriculum? The curriculum should give a strong theoretical and practical basis in the subject. It should enable to cultivate in students of library science leadership, enterprenuership, information culture and relational abilities. The students also should get necessary training insolving information problems and for total change of the management of information for the organisations where they ought to work. But these factors are seldom taken into account in the curriculum development in library science schools in India.

In respect of contents of various levels of courses in

library science, we still give more importance to traditional subjects in library science. The subjects that have no practical application in real work situations are included. Some of the library science schools are adding new topics in each paper and reluctant to scrape down anything from the existing content and so each paper will contain more topics than what the students can study within the allotted time. Some of the library schools are even reluctant to include new topics in the syllabi. In some of the library schools the curriculum is the mix of the traditional core discipline with information technology. All these adversely affect the manpower produced in library schools in one way or other. A uniform syllabus which is need-based with a practical problem solving orientation is more appropriate for the library science schools in developing countries like India.

In respect of instructional methods in library schools, age-old lecture method is still prevalent. New teaching methods, teaching tools are still to be evolved. Group discussion, seminar, tutorials is seldom adopted. Using modern information technology tools for teaching is still a remote idea in majority of the library schools. Innovation in teaching methods should become more important. Teaching should be more student centred than teacher-centred. More thrust should be given by teachers to students for learning rather than teaching.

Examination evaluation methods are not always objective and full proof due to the existing system or due to the laxity of the examiners to perform the evaluation more objectively. Age-old examination system inherited from the British system of evaluation introduced in India to test the memory of the students within a specified period of 3 hours is totally unscientific to measure the real and relative capability and caliber of students. Measures should be taken to evaluate the ability of students by other methods like giving assignments, seminars, tutorials, group discussion. In this respect equal emphasis should be given to internal assessment and written examination. Objective type and short answer type questions have to be included more in the question papers in order to evaluate the answers of the students more objectively.

CONCLUSION

It is appropriate to quote Abrahamson in the article “Diseases of the curriculum”. He pointed out a number of diseases infecting in the curriculum such as curriculo-sclerosis, arthritis, ossification, hypertrophy of the curriculum, carcinoma, curricular dysesthesia, essential curriculities, latrogenous and curricular psychosis. On examination of the curriculum of library science schools in Third world countries in general and India in particular, it is found that the treatment of the aforesaid diseases and to rejuvenate the curriculum are the needs of the hour. Design of a requirement-based curriculum is needed in library science. The design of specialised courses in Information technology is imperative to meet the manpower requirements of the future libraries. This would help to prepare future information professionals for the 21st century. This would also help to prepare future information professionals for identifying the kinds of capabilities and confidence they must have to excel in their given profession. If the library schools do not do any thing for revamping the curriculum in tune with the time to produce the need-based manpower in the field, the information professionals in the 21st centuary will face a tough competition from professional from other fields such as Computer Science, Communication, Lingustics and Management Science. Of course, survival of the fittest is the rule of the nature!

REFERENCES

1. Devarajan.G: Library Science education and manpower. New Delhi, ESS ESS, 1995.
2. Deschatelets, Giles: Opening LIS curricula to the new worlds of electronic strategic information.FID Bulletin 47(1)1997
3. Kent, Allen and Lancour, Harold, Ed: Encyclopeadia of Library and Information Science. New York, Marcel Dekker & inc.V.6 P.373.
4. ibid.p.373
5. Tejomurthy, A,Ed: Restructuring of library and Information Science curriculum.New Delhi,Concept,1994
6. UNESCO: World Information Report, 1998.Unesco, 1997.P 43.

Chapter 11

Parameters in Qualitative Research in LIS

INTRODUCTION

The major objectives of a university are teaching, publication and extension activities. All these functions are interrelated and helpful in achieving successful development and rating of universities. Of these, research is the core function, which radiates and influences the other objectives of a university.

Withelm Von Humboldt, the German thinker, recognized the importance of research in universities. The concept of "Research University" was initiated with the founding of Berlin University in 1810. This concept found fulfillment in the American research-oriented universities like John Hopkins, Stanford and Berkeley.

Research in Indian universities at an organized level was started only after independence. Now all universities undertake academic research leading to research degrees such as Ph.D. M.Litt and D.Litt. There is much apprehension among educationists and others concerned with research and development in India whether the quality of research is maintained in the true sense of the term.

Quality research is a relative concept. How is the quality of research determined or measured is now a topic of discussion and great concern in academic circle. It is a grim fact that the quality of research is declining especially in university level research. It is indeed essential that the research output should be capable of developing theoretical foundation of the subject and it should contain suggestions as to how to solve problems relating to the subject in the contemporary society and for all round societal development. But most of the university level researches in India have become more or less rituals and mere academic exercises. Who is responsible for this situation? Researchers? Research Guides? University authorities? Or the Government? We cannot attribute the blame to any one of them because all of them are responsible for this state of affairs. The decline in quality research is due to a number of interrelated factors. The main factor may be the resource crunch in the field of higher education especially in Third world countries as pointed out in the World Education Report (1998). Of course, it is high time to examine with open mind how to improve the quality of research within the parameters and by exploiting the existing infrastructure and other resources available in our universities. It is needless to state that revamping of research is imperative and it is more significant especially in the era of information technology and a society rapidly moving towards what is called information society. Attempts can be made to improve the quality of research in the area of Library and Information Science in our universities. Of course, there is no single way. Immediate attention is imperative for the qualitative improvement of research in library & Information Science.

TENETS FOR QUALITATIVE RESEARCH

Attention in the following areas may be considered for an effective and meaningful research in Library and

Information Science in Indian universities.

CONDUCT OF PERIODICAL WORKSHOPS TO RESEARCH GUIDES AND RESEARCHERS

Workshops may be conducted in all universities in India for research students as well as research guides. Separate workshops may be conducted for Research Guides and Research students. The course content of the workshop should include topics like:

a) Literature search which includes Manual literature search, CD-ROM information search, On-line information search and INTERNET search; b) Technical writing-modern techniques in preparing these and dissertations; introduction to various style manual; evaluation of research reports etc.; and c) Application of statistical techniques in data analysis. The period of workshop can be one to two weeks and this may be conducted periodically based on the requirements of research registrants.

QUALIFYING EXAMINATION

A qualifying examination may be conducted for research students when they complete one year after registration. There can be two examination papers of 3 hours duration. Each paper should carry 100 marks. The papers may be in i) Literature search & Technical writing; and ii) Research Methodology and Statistical methods. Questions should be framed in such a way as to ascertain the real aptitude of the researcher. Students who secure 60% minimum marks only may be permitted to continue research.

GRADING SYSTEM IN EVALUATION

In the evaluation of thesis grading system may be

introduced. While recommending for awarding Ph.D or other research degrees the system of Grading A, B, C (corresponding to Excellent, Very Good and Good) etc can be followed. This can be recorded in the certificate so that it will serve as a motivation for researchers as well as research guides and will make them more conscious in im0roving the quality.

IDENTIFICATION OF THRUST AREAS OF RESEARCH.

Research committee in each Department should prepare a list of research topics in the field of study as thrust areas, which have theoretical, practical and social relevance and contemporary significance. The selections of topic from this list will avoid repetitive and parallel researches and pave way for relay research.

INFRASTRUCTURE

Adequate infrastructure such as laboratory, library, manpower and physical facilities are necessary for quality research. To ensure this a committee in each Department or the research committee in each university should examine these aspects periodically in detail, objectively and without bias.

DATABASES ON RESEARCH

Each university should take steps for the creation of two databases in research viz.

i) Research already completed and degree was awarded; and

ii) Research in progress in each university. This will avoid duplication of research and repetitive research among universities and give way for productive research.

FOREIGN ADJUDICATORS

In earlier days most of the universities in India have engaged foreign adjudicatiors for valuation of theses. But now most of the universities have dispensed with foreign examiners due to delay in getting back the report duly evaluated. Delay in getting the report is not a problem today because of the advent of information technology. The authorities may be willing to accept E-mail report and digital signature of the adjudicator. The foreign examiners by and large will evaluate theses objectively and without any bias. But if we depend only on Indian evaluators we cannot expect an evaluated report without bias. Today, in most of the cases the evaluation is done more or less on a mutual agreement among Guides. This will lead to decline in the quality of research. Hence inclusion of at least one foreign evaluator in the panel of adjudicators for valuation is necessary.

AWARDS TO RESEARCH GUIDES AND RESEARCHERS

Each university may institute awards to research guides and to researchers on the basis of research output. This can be made every year on the basis of research output assessed by an expert committee constituted by the respective university.

RESEARCH OUTPUT ON INTERNET

The research output of each university may be brought under the INTERNET by creating website. The bibliographical information about the theses along with informative abstract of each thesis should be made available to the INTERNET users at the global level.

RESEARCH AUDIT

Every university should undertake periodical research

audit by engaging experts. External members from other universities may be appointed in order to make an impartial audit of the research output of a university.

The intelligent use of information tools in transforming higher education requires that there should be changes in the concept and approaches to the present day research. In the national policy on Education document it is observed, "in the context of unprecedented explosion of knowledge, higher education has to become dynamic as never before, constantly entering uncharted areas". It may be presumed that globalization would discharge repetitive research and encourage research workers to become more participative and collaborative with their peers working elsewhere. The application of IT will help in the selection of research topics and will avoid duplication of research and the spending of time unnecessarily for literature survey. The universities in India should become aware of the immense possibilities of IT in rejuvenating and improving the quality of research. If we hesitate to take timely action in this regard we will lag far behind in the quality of research. An earnest effort is imperative from researchers, research guides and university authorities to improve the quality of research as part of Total Quality Management (TQM) in higher education.

CHECKLIST FOR THE EVALUATION OF A THESIS

The value of a thesis is determined on the basis of its quality. But, how can the Quality be assessed since the concept itself is a relative and a nebulous one. There is no prescribed standard available in the field of research to determine the quality of research. However, some of the guidelines or checklist available to the researchers are those suggested by experts in the field. These checklists can be used as criteria to assess the quality of research. Of course, the objective evaluation of theses is very essential for the qualitative improvement of research. Hence it is imperative on the part of the adjudicators of thesis to follow the checklist or guidelines laid down by experts for objective and unbiased evaluation of thesis and for ensuring this as one of the means of qualitative improvement in the field of research.

GUIDELINES FOR THE EVALUATION OF RESEARCH STUDIES

The following are some of the significant studies in which guidelines are formulated by experts in the field for evaluation of research studies.

In a study entitled "Thesis and assignment writing" Anderson and others suggested the following guidelines for the evaluation of research studies. The guidelines are broadly grouped under five heads viz Problem, Design, Procedure, Analysis and Conclusion. A total of 25 guidelines are provided... There are five guidelines (1-5) under the head problem. Nine guidelines (6-13) are provided under research design. There are four guidelines (15-18) provided under data gathering procedure listed under the head Procedure. The methods that are to be followed in the analysis of data are given under two guidelines (19-20) under the head Analysis. The head "conclusion" includes five guidelines (21-25). The specific guidelines are given under.

1. Is the problem clearly stated?
2. Is the problem significant - will the results contribute to the solution of some practical or theoretical problem?
3. Are the hypotheses clearly stated?
4. Are the hypotheses logically deduced from some theory or problem?
5. Is the relationship to previous research made clear?

6. Are the assumptions of the study clearly stated?
7. Are the limitations of the study stated?
8. Are important terms in the study defined?
9. Is the research design fully described?
10. Is the research design appropriate?
11. Are the population and sample described?
12. Is the method of sampling appropriate?
13. Are the controls described and appropriate?
14. Is the research design free of specific weaknesses?
15. Are the data gathering methods described?
16. Are the data gathering methods appropriate?
17. Are the data gathering methods properly used?
18. Are the validity and reliability of the evidence established?
19. Are the analysis methods appropriate and are they properly applied?
20. Are the results of the analysis clearly presented?
21. Are the conclusions clearly stated?
22. Are the conclusions substantiated by the evidence presented?
23. Are the generalizations confined to the population from which sample was drawn?
24. Is the report logically organized and clearly written?
25. Is the tone of the report impartial and scientific?

Guruswarny and Jayaraman in their study entitled "Evaluation of research" state that the following guidelines may be used as instrument for evaluating research report.

There are nineteen guidelines. The evaluation should concentrate on the aspects such as title, prefatory materials included, problem raised, previous works cited, objectives stated, hypothesis formulated, assumptions made, concepts defined, problem studied, sample design, tools used, procedure followed in research, safeguard taken, evidence presented and analyzed, summary and conclusions, limitations recognized, further works projected, bibliography and appendix and report, format and style used in the report.

In the study "Methodology of educational research" Koul has suggested the following guidelines for evaluation of research studies. The major areas focused in the research study for evaluation include the preliminary section, body of the report, (includes introduction, design of the study, analysis and interpretation of the data, summary and conclusions); and reference section. The preliminary section provides five guidelines, which focus on title, preface, table of contents, list of tables, and list of figures. The body of the report includes 18 guidelines focused specifically on introduction, design of the study, analysis and interpretation of the data and summary and conclusions. The reference section constitutes three guidelines that are specifically focused on Bibliography, appendix and index, if any

In the study entitled "How to complete your research project successfully" Judith Bell has formulated 23 guidelines as instrument to evaluate research studies. The guidelines include aspects relating to clarity of the language, references, title of the study, objective of the study, hypothesis, literature review, data collection method, limitations of the study, statistical technique used, data analysis, visuals used in the study, recommendations, appendix etc.

In the book "Research Methods in Library and

Information Science", Krishan Kumar brings out a set of criteria for the evaluation of research report. He has also given a set of criteria for evaluation of completed research reports. These criteria are grouped under general format, Research title, Statement of the problem, Hypotheses, Objectives of the study, Assumptions and Limitations, Review of Related Literature, Research design of the study, Collection of Data, Presentation of data, Analysis of data, Interpretation of data, Summary and Conclusions. General scholarship, Bibliography and Appendices are also taken as areas that are to be considered for assessing the value of the research report.

Busha and Harter in their study have formulated the following guidelines for the objective evaluation of a research study.

1. What are the conclusions of the research?
2. Does the study answer the research question posed?
3. Is the methodology adequate for the research problem under investigation?
4. Have assumptions been explicitly identified and are they reasonable and acceptable?
5. Are the instruments or indexes used by the investigator adequate reflections of the conceptual variables of the study?
6. If a rest or experiment was conducted as a part of the research, are the results sufficiently conclusive so that the hypotheses can be accepted as tentative, theoretical knowledge or put to practical use?
7. Can conclusions of the study be generalized to a larger population?
8. Are the conclusions linked to other assertions so that findings can be incorporated into existing theory?

9. What was the hypothesis or the research question?
10. Was the hypothesis of social or theoretical significance and was the problem stated so that it can be solved?
11. What are the independent and dependent variables of the research?
12. Did investigators appear to be aware of any intervening variables, and, if so, how did the researchers account for them?
13. What are the theoretical implications of research? Did the researcher appear to be aware of them?
14. Were graphical or tabular formats appropriately used to display pertinent data?
15. If sampling procedures were used, were they adequately explained in the research report?
16. If the investigator claimed to have selected a random sample, was it actually chosen so that each member of the population had an equal chance of being selected?
17. Was the methodology explained in an understandable manner so that it can be easily replicated?
18. What techniques were used to analyze quantitative or qualitative data? Were these techniques appropriate for the investigation?
19. Did the investigator conduct a literature search prior to the Project's initiation? If so, was the study then related to past, similar investigations?
20. Did the investigator make recommendations for future study?
21. Was the research report written in a factual, straightforward, honest, and lucid manner, and was it free of incorrect grammar, spelling errors, and

emotionally laden words and phrases?

Analytical approach to the criteria for the Evaluation of Thesis.

From an analytical approach to the guidelines formulated above by various experts it can be seen that the guidelines range from 20 to 25. Also all these guidelines are focused on various regions or aspects of the report such as preliminary, main body of the report or text and auxiliaries. Based on the guidelines proposed by various authors a checklist is deducted below for an objective and unbiased evaluation of Ph.D thesis.

STRUCTURAL ORGANISATION OF THE THESIS

A thesis should ensure a structural organization in order viz Preliminaries, the Main body or the Text and Auxiliaries. Hence the evaluator should consider whether the investigator has maintained this aspect succinctly in the report.

PRELIMINARIES

The items of information contained in the preliminaries are title page of the thesis, preface or acknowledgement, declaration, contents page and list of tables and figures. The title of the thesis is an important component to be evaluated. Whether the title expresses subject clearly and co-extensive with the subject investigated in the study? Have other information such as statement of authorship, institution affiliation and year of submission etc been included in the title page. In the case of contents page, whether it serves as the mirror of the report. In the case of list of tables and figures, whether the details given about the tables and figures are self explanatory and expressive, and necessary index numbers are given for locating these without much effort.

THE BODY OR THE TEXT OF THE THESIS

This is the main area of the study that should be subjected for objective evaluation. The following aspects are to be considered for evaluation.

1. Problem of the Study

Whether the topic or the problem selected for study is current, significant, relevant and capable to solve theoretical and or practical problems in the filed of study? Is definition of the significant concepts in the title of the topic clearly given?

2. Objective of the Study

Whether the investigator has succeeded in formulating the objective/s pertinent to the study? Here, the evaluator so as to justify the objectivity should ascertain the main objective and sub objectives.

3. Hypothesis

Are the hypotheses formulated in the study relevant to the topic and do they form a basis for theory? Whether the investigator was successful in combining the variables logically and clearly in formulating the hypothesis?

4. Research Design & Research Methodology

The study should be evaluated in relation to research methodology and research design under the following aspects.

Is/are the research methodology/ies used in the study adequately described? Is the research design appropriate to the study? Are the population, sample described and sampling appropriate? Are the controls used appropriately and is the research design free from any weakness. Are the data gathering methods described, appropriate and, properly used in the conduct of study?

5. Review of Related Studies

Whether the study is well documented with review of related studies conducted by the investigator as part of literature survey? Has adequate support or linkage been made in the thesis with that of studies conducted earlier.

6. Limitations of Study

Whether the study has spelt out the limitations if any imposed by the investigator? Are the limitations considered logical and appropriate to the topic of the study?

7. Data Analysis

The thesis should be evaluated against the data analysis carried out in the study. Whether the investigator has used scientific and statistical techniques for the analysis of quantitative and qualitative data? Whether the investigator tried for in-depth analysis of data. The correctness of the equations and inferences made should also be ascertained.

8. Level of Interpretation

Proper interpretation of the data is also another important aspect to be considered for the evaluation of a research study. Whether logical interpretations are made by the investigator during the analysis of the data?

9. Findings

Whether the investigator has succeeded in bringing out the findings of the study in relation to the objectives laid down? Whether the findings substantiate the hypothesis formulated in the study?

10. Testing of Hypothesis & Conclusion

The study is also to be evaluated in terms of whether the investigator has attempted testing of the validity of the hypothesis either conceptually or statistically?

11. Area of Future Research

Whether the investigator has suggested any areas of research in future? Are the topics suggested by the investigator relevant and significant?

12. Language

The thesis should also be evaluated in terms of language used. The aspects such as clarity, grammar, spelling, diction, readability norms, coherence etc should also be considered in evaluation.

13. Visuals

Whether the visuals used in the thesis are appropriate, complete and free from errors?

AUXILIARIES

The areas under the auxiliaries to be evaluated are mainly references, and appendix. Whether the references are relevant, complete? Whether the style manual for rendering references is consistently followed? Whether appendices are numbered and proper headings are given?

CONCLUSION

Of course guidelines are useful in the evaluation of a thesis scientifically. A thesis with good structural organisation, objectivity of the content, good visuals and documentation, clarity of language and free from aberrations will be well rated. The scientific and systematic evaluation of thesis will enable to enhance the standard of research output and thereby to make qualitative improvement of research in the academic institutions.

REFERENCES

1. Anderson, et al : Thesis and assignment writing. New Delhi, Wiley Eastern,1971
2. Bell, Judith : How to complete your research project successfully. New Delhi, UBSPD,,1993.
3. Busha, Charles H and Harter, Stephen H: Research methods in librarianship: techniques and interpretations. New York, Academic Press, 1988.
4. Devarajan.G: Library and Information Science education and manpower. New Delhi, ESS ESS, 1995.
5. Guruswamy, PA and Jayaraman, R: Evaluation of research reports. In Handbook of methodology of research ed.by Rajammal P Devadas. Coimbatore . SriRamakrishna Mission Vidhyalaya Teacher's college, 1976.
6. Krishan Kumar: Research methods in Library & Information Science, New Delhi, Viksa, 1999
7. Koul, Lokesh: Methodology of educational research.New Delhi, Vikas, 1997.
8. Verma.G.K and Beard.R.M: What is educational research? Hants, Gower, 1981.

Bibliography

Ackoff, RL: Towards a behavioural theory of communication. Management Science.4.pp.218-34.

Akst, D : The digital library : Its future has arrived. Carnegie Reporter.2(3) PP.4-8

Anderson, et al : Thesis and assignment writing. New Delhi, Wiley Eastern,1971

Anderson, Verna Divkman : "Reading and Young Children", London, Macmillan,1968.

Andretta, Susie and Cutting, Andrew: Information literacy: A plug- and-play approach.Libri.53(3)2003.pp202-209.

Association of Indian Universities (New Delhi). New education policy. New Delhi, AUI,1985.

Bell, Judith : How to complete your research project successfully. New Delhi, UBSPD,1997

Bhattacharyya,G: Information Science : A unified view through a system approach. Calcutta, IASLIC, 1978.

Bloss, Meredith: Responding to manifest needs. Library Journal.89(16)1964

Borko, H: Information Science: What is it? American Documentation. January, 1968.

Bose,H: Information Science: Principles and practice. New Delhi, Sterling, 1986.

Bound, Goy L, et al: "Reading Difficulties their Diagnosis and Connection" N.J.Prentice Hall,1979. Busha, Charles H and Harter, Stephen H: Research methods in librarianship: Techniques and interpretations. New York, Academic Press, 1988.

Candela, L, et al: The DELOS digital library reference model - foundations for digital libraries. version 0.98 February 2008.

Centre for Research in Library and Information Management (Manchester): Conference Proceedings on Libraries without walls, 17-20 September, 1997.

Compaine, Benjamin M ,Ed. The digital divide: Facing a crisis or creating a myth? Cambridge, MIT Press,2001.

Corbin, Lisa: Speeding up the data: Superhighway. Observer. 31January,1996

Davenport, Thomas: Information ecology: Mastering the Information and knowledge environment. New York, OUP,1979.

Deschatelets, Giles: Opening LIS curricula to the new worlds of electronic strategic information.FID Bulletin 47(1)1997

Desidoc: Sanjay User Guide. New Delhi, Desidoc, 1991.

Devarajan G : "Impact of socio-economic Factors on the Reading Habits of Students in the Secondary Schools Students", (ICSSR Project), Trivandrum, University of Kerala,1992.

Devarajan,G,Ed: Bibliometric studies. New Delhi, ESS ESS, 1997.

Devarajan.G., Information Technology in libraries, New Delhi, Ess Ess Publications, 1999.

Devarajan.G: Library Science education and manpower. New Delhi, ESS ESS, 1995.

Edward A Fox: The digital libraries initiative -update and discussion, Bulletin of the American Society of Information Science.26(1)1999.

Eisenberg, Michael B, et al : Information literacy : Essential skills for the information age.London Libraries Unlimited, 2005.

Emory University, Atlanta: Virtual library project. Atlanta, Emory University, 1994.

Encyclopedia Britanica.ed.15.v.6-Micropedia.Chicago, Encyclopedia Britanica Inc. 1993.

Fitzimmons,J: Information technology and third industrial revolution. Electronic library. 12(5)94pp.295-97.

Ganesh Natarajan and Sandhya Shkhar. Knowledge management: Enabling business growth. New Delhi, McGraw Hill , 2000.

Gertz, Janet: Selection for preservation in the digital age. Library Resources & Technical services.44(2) 2000.PP. 97-104

Gopinathan S. : "A Measure of Reading", IE Survey of Reading Interest and Habits, Singapore Institution of Education,1978.

Guruswamy, PA and Jayaraman, R: Evaluation of research reports. In Handbook of methodology of research ed.by Rajammal P Devadas. Coimbatore . SriRamakrishna Mission Vidhyalaya Teacher's college, 1976.

Harrod's Librarians' Glossary of terms used in librarianship documentation, and the book crafts and reference Book. Ed.5.USA, Gower Pub.Co.1984..

Hawkins, BL(199) Distribute learning and institutional restructuring. Educom.Review 34(4)1999.

Heinish. C : Cyberlib: Vision and economic analysis. Libri. 44 (4)1994.p.393-99.

Homann, B: Difficulties and new approaches in user education in Germany .The Hague, IFLA,2001.

James, J: Library systems evaluation guide .v8.Ohio, Rush Associates, 1980

Kahn, RE and Cerf, VG : The digital library project vol.1 - The world of knowbots,1988.

Kamalavijayan D: Information and knowledge management. Delhi, Macmillan India,2005

Kent, Allen and Lancour, Harold, Ed: Encyclopedia of Library and Information Science. New York, Marcel Dekker & inc.1961.

Koch, M: Information Literacy: Where do we go from here? Techno quarterly for Education and Technolgy.10(1) 2003.

Koehler, AEC: Some thoughts on the meaning of open access for university library .Technical services serials review. 32(1)2006

Koul, Lokesh: Methodology of educational research. New Delhi,Vikas,1997.

Krishan Kumar: Reference Service.ed.4.New Delhi, Vikas, 1991.

Krishan Kumar: Research methods in Library & Information Science, New Delhi, Vikas, 1999

Kumar, PSG: Fundamentals of Information Science. New Delhi.S.Chand and Co.,1998.

Lee. H.W.: Networked, electronic and virtual library: Libraries of the 1990s.Jl.of Educational Media and Library sciences. 32(2)95.p.119-29

Lybsys: Pamphlet. New Delhi, Lybsys Corporation

Machlup,F and Mansfield,U: Study of information, interdisciplinary messages. New York, Wiley.1983.

Malwad,N.M.,et al, ed: Digital libraries: Dynamic store house of digitised information. New Delhi, New Age International, 1996.

Malwad.N.M: Selection criteria for library automation software. Desidoc Bulletin.15 (2) 1995.p.17-25.

Martin, William: The global information society. London, Aslib, 1995.

McGarry,KJ: Changing context of information: An introductory analysis. London, Clive Bingly.1981.

McGlammery.P.: Magic at the University of Connecticut: Building the virtual map library Geography and map division Bulletin.179.1995.p.14-30.

Mckee, Bob: Information studies. Libr. Ass. Rec. 1986. 88(5) pp. 236-39.

Molhot,Pat: The nature of information and its influence on libraries. Special Libraries. July 1984.p.247.

Neelameghan, A: Information technology and rural development. Information Studies4(1)1988.pp.55-61

Pejova, Z: Information literacy: An issue which requests urgent action in developing countries and countries in transition. Prague, Unesco,2003.

Polley.J.A. and Lyon.E: out of the archives and into the street: American memory in American libraries. Online. 16(5)1992.p.51-57.

Prasher,RG: Information and communication. ILA Bulletin 23(3)1987.p.18.

Prytherch, Ray: Information Management and Library Science: A guide to the literature. Aldershot, Gower,1994.

Rader HB: Information literacy: An emerging global priority, Prague, Unesco, 2002.

Rajagopalan,T: Some issues in higher education. The Hindu, 9th March.p.22.

Rojas, B A: Information systems for the Scientific Management of Agricultural Research - Conference on selected issues of Agricultural Research in Latin America. Madrid,1982.Isnar.March, 1981

Rowley, Jennifer E: The basics of information technology. London, Clive Bingly, 1988.

Sarada. K: Rural library services in India. New Delhi, ESS ESS, 1986.

Sathyanarayana, R: Information Technology and its facets. New Delhi, Manak,1996.

Sathyanarayana.M: Public library and community analysis. New Delhi, Reliance Publishing House, 1997.

Seghal.R.L: Handbook of library software packages. New Delhi, ESS ESS, 1998.

Sharma, Pandey S.K: Libraries and Society. New Delhi, ESS ESS. 1992.

Shera,JH: The foundation of education for librarianship. New York, Becker & Hayes, 1972.

Singhal R.P. : "Indian Schools : A study of Teacher Pupil Relation", New Delhi, Vikas,1988.

Staiger, Ralph, Ed : "The Teaching of Reading", Paris, Unesco,,1979.

Tejomurthy, A,Ed: Restructuring of library and Information Science curriculum.New Delhi,Concept,1994

The World Bank: World Development report: Knowledge for

Development, 1998-99 New York, OUP Press.2002

Unesco: World information report, 1997-98.Paris, Unesco.1998

University of Illinois Committee on Institutional Cooperation, USA: Creating a virtual electronic library.Van Nostrand's Scientific Encyclopeadia. Ed.8.New York, Van Nostrand's and Reinhold.1994.

Vasistha K.K. : "Teacher Education in India", New Delhi, Concept,1979.

Vengan.R., *et al,Ed.* Caliber-2000: Information Services in a networked environment in India. Ahmedabad, Inflibnet Centre, 2000.

Verma.G.K and Beard.R.M: What is educational research? Hants, Gower, 1981.

Webster's New Encyclopedia. New York, Printice Hall, 1992.

Whitehead, MJ and Quilan, CA: Canada: An information literacy case study.

Wikipedia. http://en.wikipedia.org

William, William F: Principles of automated information retrieval. Illinois, Business press, 1965.

Yovits, MC: Information Science: Towards the development of a true scientific discipline. American Documentation. 20, 1969.

Zorkoczy, P and Heap, N : Information Technology. ed. 4. London, Pitman. 1995.

Index

A

B

C

D